Children in Treatment

Children in Treatment

A Primer for Beginning Psychotherapists

by

SHIRLEY COOPER, M.S.

Chief Psychiatric Social Worker,
Department of Psychiatry

and

LEON WANERMAN, M.D.

Associate Chief,
Department of Psychiatry

Mount Zion Hospital and Medical Center,
San Francisco

BRUNNER/MAZEL, *Publishers* • New York

Library of Congress Cataloging in Publication Data

Cooper, Shirley
   Children in treatment.

   Includes bibliographies.
   1. Child psychotherapy. I. Wanerman, Leon joint author.
II. Title.
RJ504.C62   618.9'28'914   77-7637
ISBN 0-87630-144-8 (hard cover)
ISBN 0-87630-333-5 (paperback)

Published by
BRUNNER/MAZEL, INC.
19 Union Square West
New York, New York 10003

MANUFACTURED IN THE UNITED STATES OF AMERICA

10 9 8 7 6 5

To Paddy and Sol and our children,
with love

Foreword

This book is a delight to read because it provides so many vignettes with so many insights into the feelings and anxieties, conflicts and motives of children in treatment. It is invaluable to the trainee and child therapist from all the mental health professions. The setting from which the training model is taken is essentially a psychoanalytic one and focuses on a particular developmental approach. This approach does not include some of the issues in development, especially related to cognitive, psychosocial and psychophysiological or neurological integration. On the other hand the ego-psychological approach coupled with the detailed understanding of individual psychology on a developmental basis is very crucial to the development of the understanding of children. That particular combination of theoretical approaches to child psychotherapy is often missing in some of the programs. The very practical principles of engaging a child in treatment, how to ask the right questions, etc., are very helpful to beginning students as is a discussion of toys and play.

The diagnostic assessments which give one some sense of why different children react to the efforts to understand their problem are very instructive to the reader. The particular role of psychological testing in diagnostic assessment is nicely delineated as are the other kinds of assessments which might be helpful in a good clinical evaluation. The book concludes with a chapter on understanding and working with parents which shows a variety of ways of working with parents, gained from many years of experience.

This book is both a very practical and enjoyable way of being introduced to many of the vicissitudes with which the trainee in child therapy is confronted. The many examples that are given of how one handles a variety of the issues are extremely supportive and heartening to the trainee readers. I am certain that many who are experienced in working with children will also enjoy and profit from, as I from the experience of reading CHILDREN IN TREATMENT.

IRVING N. BERLIN, M.D.
Professor of Psychiatry and Pediatrics,
Vice Chairman for Child Mental Health,
University of California at Davis;
President of The American Academy of
*   Child Psychiatry*

Contents

Introduction

There is a certain type of client who creates special problems in the administration of social agencies and in the interviewing situation. The client seems totally unable to comprehend the function of a social agency. He frequently creates disorder and chaos in the waiting room. Often he talks loudly and shrilly, demanding numerous attentions, and has been known to look boldly over the shoulder of a typist as she transcribes confidential reports. In the initial interview with the caseworker, this client states more or less positively that he has no problem and he does not know why he had come to the agency. Further difficulties are encountered when it appears that he cannot sit in a chair for more than five minutes. He tends to concentrate on irrelevant matters like the operation of the venetian blinds, the counting of squares on the asphalt tile floors, the manipulation of paper clips into abstract forms.

The client has neither marital problems nor employment problems. He is not in need of relief, although he will gladly take a hand-out. The sex of the client may be male or female. The age is roughly five to fifteen years. What shall we do with him?*

What indeed shall we do with this group of perplexing patients? Experienced child clinicians continue to seek for ever better ways of helping troubled children and their families, while therapists who come to work with children for the first time discover these questions anew.

In the course of years of helping to educate new therapists, we have tried to prepare them for their first meetings with children and families. Our experience in the Children's Service of the Depart-

---

*Fraiberg, Selma H. (1952), Some Aspects of Casework with Children: Part I. *Social Casework*, Vol. 33, No. 9, p. 374.

ment of Psychiatry at Mount Zion Hospital and Medical Center (San Francisco) has persuaded us that mental health trainees of all disciplines can profit from some orientation to psychotherapeutic work with children. The teaching staff has struggled with how to approach the problem of preparing students for their beginning work. We have been concerned with what attitudes to convey, what content to include, how extensive preparation and orientation should be, and how best to translate complex theoretical ideas into sound principles of beginning practice. Each academic year, we have tinkered with inclusions and deletions, modifications and clarifications of our orientation manual, which is used in a series of introductory seminars. This version is a further extension and generalization which, we hope, can be useful to other training centers.

Current knowledge of human psychology and child development is an admixture of some more-or-less hard data. It is organized around concepts, speculations, observations, inferences, experiences and some frank guesses. All of this we call "theory." As with all theories—even the best of them—reality is only approximated. For a theory to be useful, it must be a living and changing entity, capable of being altered in response to new discoveries and experiences. However, imperfect as our theoretical understanding is, it stands as a model of clarity when compared to our principles of practice. The road between how to understand and what to do is still largely uncharted. Nonetheless, our experience suggests that some introduction to practice based upon currently held theory, is important for the beginning clinician. Without this, the beginner is left with no guideposts, and is obliged to reinvent the proverbial wheel.

However, regardless of the preparation provided, the beginner faces a fundamental problem. Ideally, the novice needs to know everything. Since this is both absurd and impossible, beginners are obliged to take considerable information on faith. They must not only absorb a great deal in a relatively short time, but also convey a task-oriented therapeutic approach when both the task and the means to achieve it remain unclear.

The corollary problem for the teacher is the need to select information which will neither overload the student nor offer so many injunctions as to crowd out initiative and inventiveness. The ghost of the teacher must not pervade the playroom. Thus, advice, information and preparation must be tempered to permit judicious experimentation while forewarning the novice about common pitfalls. Despite the teacher's efforts, the new clinician cannot, for example, fully comprehend that over-reassurance or too rapid gratification can impair the treatment work, when children pull for such responses naturally. Nor can the teacher anticipate the extensive and creative variations of these natural impulses to reassure and gratify. Frequently, the new clinician will convert tact into "pussyfooting." Being direct is often confused with becoming directive. Excesses of empathy may become rationalizations for ignoring important material or avoiding confronting maladaptive behaviors. Nor is it simple to convey to the beginning therapist that he may be important to the patient when the novice is feeling "all thumbs."

Despite these problems, we have been encouraged by the responses of our students and those colleagues who have asked to use our orientation materials in their teaching efforts. This led to the decision to revise and expand our prior efforts into this "primer" for beginners.

Throughout this volume, we make certain assumptions about those who begin their work as child psychotherapists. One assumption is that the reader will have some theoretical background in child development, psychodynamics and psychopathology. There is much excellent literature on these vast subjects which we will not recapitulate here in more than a superficial review. Furthermore, we assume that most clinicians beginning their work with children have had some prior experience with the psychotherapy of adults. Therefore, general principles of psychotherapeutic techniques are not presented except as they relate specifically to the beginning treatment of children. In addition, the appreciation of diverse cultural and socioeconomic factors and their important implications for effective clinical work cannot be overstated, and we assume some familiarity with such knowledge.

Finally, we assume that most of our readers will be receiving some training in their ongoing work with their child patients. This training will provide help, over time, with learning the details and refinements of psychotherapeutic technique. Such training is essential to the mastery of clinical work since we doubt that any book—including this one—could replace supervised experience.

In this volume we attempt to integrate theory and long-term psychotherapeutic methodology and technique. The book introduces the novice child psychotherapist to the world of children. It attempts to review simply some of the major ideas the beginning worker will need to keep in mind. It offers practical suggestions and advice about how to proceed in the beginning phases of clinical work with children and families. These suggestions have been supported, wherever possible, by principles and rationales so that the reader has some basis for judging their sense and utility.

To demonstrate these principles in action, we have used as many illustrations as possible. Whenever we could, we have let the children speak for themselves, in words and drawings. Other illustrations are drawn from case vignettes and case reports, most of which represent the work of our students. As samples of beginners' work, they sometimes reflect awkward as well as highly creative efforts. This kind of learning must involve errors, which are often highly instructive—albeit painful. The beginning clinician may be reassured—as our students frequently are—by the discovery that other beginners share the same apprehensions and make the same mistakes. In any event, the beginner should be encouraged by the understanding that when the psychotherapeutic "music" is well composed, the "lyric" need not be perfect. Child and adult patients have shown all of us, repeatedly, their capacity to tolerate and forgive blunders, continuing their efforts to instruct and work with us, provided that the therapeutic relationship is humane, purposeful and compassionate.

The book is divided into three major sections. The first addresses the developmental perspective necessary to the understanding of work with children and families. It portrays the basic philosophy underlying the technique and objectives in helping children and families grow and progress. It includes illustrations of many normal developmental points of stress, the understanding of which is essential in helping children.

The second section addresses common, typical and practical issues which form the context around which beginning clinical work occurs. These have been chosen from the annual round of concerns presented by our own students regarding such issues as appointment scheduling, treatment modalities, confidentiality, fees, play, toys, etc.

The third section deals with the actual beginnings of clinical work, emphasizing the diagnostic workup, the use of various aids in assessment, the problem of beginning again as in transferred cases and vacations, and some selected issues inherent in the work with parents.

We hope the children and their families presented here will come alive for the reader and, in doing so, give life to the principles we have tried to convey. We equally hope that the book will provide enjoyment as well as instruction, though we are certain that it is neither the last word nor the complete gospel.

A Note on Basic Readings

The literature on the theory and practice of treating children and their families is already vast and growing daily. Under each section, we have selected a few relevant readings. However, the beginning therapist will profit from a familiarity with some of the basic literature about child psychotherapy. Some of these sources are journals including *The Psychoanalytic Study of the Child*, the *Journal of the American Academy of Child Psychiatry*, the *Journal of the American Orthopsychiatric Association*, the *Journal of Child Psychology and Psychiatry*, *Adolescence*, and *Child Development*. A useful annual is the *Annual Progress in Child Psychiatry and Child Development* (1968-1977), edited by Stella Chess, M.D. and Alexander Thomas, M.D., New York: Brunner/Mazel. *Family Process*, the *Journal of Social Work* and *Social Casework* will frequently have useful articles on work with children and, more particularly, the treatment of families.

It is difficult to select the most relevant texts; however, the comprehensive *Bibliography of Child Psychiatry and Child Mental Health* (1976), edited by Irving Berlin, M.D., New York: Human Sciences Press, is an invaluable source.

In addition, we think the reader will value selected reports from the *Group for the Advancement of Psychiatry*, Volume II of *The American Handbook of Psychiatry* (1974), edited by Gerald Caplan, M.D., New York: Basic Books, and the *Report of the Joint Com-*

mission on the Mental Health of Children. Crisis in Child Mental Health: Challenge for the 1970's (1969), New York: Harper and Row.

ACKNOWLEDGMENTS

We wish to express our thanks to the entire staff of the Children's Service of the Department of Pscyhiatry at Mount Zion Hospital and Medical Center who have helped to shape and sharpen our thinking.

Most particularly, we are indebted to four of our colleagues. Calvin Settlage, M.D., who has been the Chief of Child Psychiatry for the past eight years and whose contributions to the theory of child development and child psychiatry are well known, provided much of the material in the Chapter on "A Developmental Approach to Mental Health Training." Joseph Afterman, M.D., who has served as the Director of Training and Child Psychiatry for many years, contributed many of the ideas in the chapter on "Toys and Play." James Pearce, Ph.D., who coordinates our Department's liaison activities with the Department of Pediatrics, contributed very greatly to the section on hospitalization as well as to the chapter on "Toys and Play." Carl Nicholls, M.S.W., a most gifted child clinician, revised one of the earlier versions of our orientation manual. Many of the ideas which he contributed helped stimulate us to expand that manual into this current volume.

The efforts of our students to learn the beginning skills of child psychotherapy have taught us much, especially since most of them knew that "learning was not child's play." For this, we are grateful. We are most thankful to our patients who tolerated our blunders and taught us more than anyone.

Special thanks are due Carole Kahler, Larry Edmonds, Jamie Hardin and, most particularly, Janice Chenin who patiently typed and retyped our many versions.

"NOBODY LISSENS TO *ME*, EITHER... 'CEPT WHEN I DON'T WANT 'EM TO."

Children in Treatment

I

THE DEVELOPMENTAL

PERSPECTIVE

1

A Developmental Approach
to Mental Health Training

The task of the mental health professional is to acquire a comprehensive body of knowledge, organized and integrated in both theoretical and practical terms, and to learn to use that knowledge in work with people of all ages and sociocultural backgrounds, in any clinical or preventive setting. This knowledge will ideally include a full awareness of human development and behavior, including: sociocultural factors (cultural heritage, social role, familial forces); biological factors (animal heritage, anatomical and physiological underpinnings, organicity); and psychological factors (personality, individual psychodynamics, family and group psychodynamics).

The following specific content areas provide an optimal basis for the organization and integration of theoretical concepts and their technical application in mental health work: 1) a detailed understanding of the psychology of the individual human being; 2) a strong developmental orientation; and 3) an emphasis on an ego-psychological approach to working with people.

THE DETAILED UNDERSTANDING OF
INDIVIDUAL PSYCHOLOGY

The individual is the functional unit in human society and, in a sense, the end product of the aforementioned sociocultural, biological and psychological determinants of development and behavior. Psychological development is shaped by the interaction of the influences of unique environment with those of genetic endowment and innate, biologically predetermined timetable for the maturation of inherent capacities. During the developmental process, the impact of environmental forces—particularly the parental and other human influences involved in socialization—comes to be represented in personality through internalization and identification. To understand the psychology of the individual in all its complexity is to understand the process and outcome of human development and the forces, internal and external, which enter into the psychodynamics of human behavior. Such an understanding is essential to the effectiveness of whatever work one undertakes in the field of mental health, from individual psychotherapy to program planning or even administration.

A DEVELOPMENTAL ORIENTATION

As a result of the accruing data from observational studies of normal development and the related emerging theoretical concepts and formulations concerning the infancy, childhood and adult years of human psychological development, a developmental orientation may be employed as a primary frame of reference for understanding, preventing and treating behavioral disorders.

a) Human psychological development continues throughout the life cycle. This means that an understanding of the phase-specific normative developmental issues, conflicts and anxieties is a key element in helping or furthering the development of an individual or group of individuals in a given age period.

b) Since the developmental view emphasizes the continuity of individual human development, the attainments of each successive phase are seen as being built upon and influenced by the outcome of the preceding phases. Underscoring the commonality of child and adult psychology, this longitudinal emphasis includes both the child and the adult as participants in the same, continuous process of development. The status of each can thus be assessed in identical terms: the degree of attainment of age-appropriate individuation and the extent of freedom from development-arresting forces in the individual and in the environment.

c) Thus, the developmental view underlines the role of environmental influences not only in the past, as it has contributed to pathologic formations, but in the present, as an ongoing factor in adaptation.

d) Similarly, the developmental view stresses the progressive, impetus-providing role of normative growth forces in the treatment of emotional disorders, as well as in the development of personality.

e) In keeping with its emphasis on the continuity of development throughout the life cycle, the developmental view also stresses the recapitulation of earlier developmental issues—however well resolved or unresolved—in later developmental phases. This idea is particularly well illustrated by separation-individuation theory. Complementing the theory of the psychosexual stages, this additional developmental theory focuses on the development of the capacity for human relationship and for adaptation, as these arise from progressive ego development and self-object differentiation.

The separation-individuation process is most crucial during the first three years of life. Nevertheless, this process continues throughout development, ending with the process of dying and death. Again, the individual confronts the issue of incremental separation and loss of important figures in his life and the correlated internalization of the development of self.

The understanding of this process of recapitulation is important to mental health work for two reasons: It provides an opportunity for a further solution of unresolved problems as a part of normal development, and it provides the professional with both access to and leverage for facilitating such solution through early preventive intervention or treatment. One can capitalize on the inherent tendency of the human organism to repeat and gain mastery over the unresolved conflicts and the unfulfilled wants of his past.

f) The developmental view emphasizes the contiguity of normal and pathologic outcomes of development—recognizing that at each stress point and phase-specific juncture, the human being strives for adaptation and mastery. In this sense, psychopathology is seen as a failure in adaptation. From this perspective, the route —the reversibility of psychopathology—while not assured, is highlighted.

g) Finally, the developmental orientation views mental illness not in the medical model of disease entities affecting developed organ systems, but in the model of functional disturbances which impair current functioning and also impede further development in one or more of its lines or aspects. The aim of treatment or other remedial interventions is thus to enhance and facilitate those developmental processes which have been arrested. From this viewpoint, then, one treats not a syndrome but a developmentally arrested individual who has participated psychologically in the formation of his psychopathology and must similarly participate in its undoing. The patient is not a passive recipient but an active partner in a mutual endeavor.

AN EGO-PSYCHOLOGICAL APPROACH

Ego psychology places the ego in the central mediating position of the personality. Rather than emphasizing one's relative helplessness in the face of animal instincts or intimidation by socioculturally determined, internalized values and prohibitions, it focuses on the potential human capacity to achieve a viable balance of forces within, and between oneself and one's environment. Stress is placed on the capacity to achieve a successful and creative adaptation. In clinical terms, ego psychology dictates that 1) one work with and through the healthy part of the ego, understanding its vulnerability both to the inner demands and repressed, unconscious conflicts and to the external demands and forces which it mediates; 2) one respect the ego's need to expand in a gradual way its capacity to deal with these inner and outer demands; and 3) one provide necessary support to the ego during this process.

Because of the relative adequacy of the ego of the adult neurotic, the value of the ego-psychological approach has only gradually been appreciated. In work with children, its importance and validity have become particularly evident. Here, the clearly underdeveloped state of the child's ego has required modifications of the adult-derived psychotherapeutic method. In essence, the child psychotherapist serves as an auxiliary ego supplementing those capacities and functions lacking in the child, but necessary to the treatment process. With their development and emergence in the child during the course of treatment, the therapist yields this supplementary function.

It has become increasingly clear that a similar orientation has equal validity in work with adults. The conceptual approach of ego psychology is proving to be immensely valuable in working with the more serious adult disturbances: neurotic character disorders, narcissistic personality disorders, borderline disorders and psychoses. At the other end of the scale, ego psychology has shown its utility in the assessment of the adequacy of early development and in the formulation of programs of prevention. An important potential outcome of the use of the developmental approach is the closer integration of training for work with adults and that with children and adolescents.

FURTHER READING

Benjamin, John (1961), The Innate and the Experiential in Child Development. In: *Lectures in Experimental Psychiary*, H. W. Brosin (Ed.), Pittsburgh, Pennsylvania: University of Pittsburgh Press.

Bowlby, John (1960), Separation Anxiety. *International Journal of Psycho-Analysis*, 41:89-113.

Buxbaum, Edith (1957), Contribution to the Psychoanalytic Knowledge of the Latency Period. *Journal of the American Orthopsychiatric Association*, 21:182-198.

Dittman, Lillian L. (1968), *Early Child Care: The New Perspectives*. New York: Atherton.

Erikson, Erik (1959), *Identity and the Life Cycle*. Psychological Issues, Monograph Series No. 1. New York: International Universities Press.

Fraiberg, Selma (1968), The Origins of Identity. *Smith College Studies in Social Work*, 38:2.

Freud, Anna (1963), The Concept of Developmental Lines. *Psychoanalytic Study of the Child*, 18:245-265.

Kleeman, James A. (1967), The Peek-A-Boo Game. *Psychoanalytic Study of the Child*, 22:239-273.

Korner, Analiese (1964), Some Hypotheses Regarding the Significance of Individual Differences at Birth for Later Development. *Psychoanalytic Study of the Child*, 19:58-72.

Mahler, Margaret (1963), Thoughts About Development and Individuation. *Psychoanalytic Study of the Child*, 18:307-324.

McDevitt, John and Settlage, Calvin (Eds.), (1971), *Separation-Individuation: Essays in Honor of Margaret S. Mahler*. New York: International Universities Press.

Perlman, Helen Harris (1965), Self-Determination: Reality or Illusion. *Social Service Review*, 34:410-421.

White, Robert (1961), *Ego and Reality in Psychoanalytic Theory*. Psychological Issues, New York: International Universities Press.

Winnicott, Donald (1953), Transitional Object and Transitional Phenomena. *International Journal of Psycho-Analysis*, 34:89-152.

2

Developmental

Stress Points

An understanding of typical stresses in normal growth is essential if one is to understand normal and pathological development. This, in turn requires that several factors be considered. S. Freud, Erikson, Mahler, A. Freud and Piaget, among others, have provided ways to conceptualize the inner forces which influence development across a lifetime. In addition, external events are another set of forces influencing development.

It is useful to examine the context in which inner forces and outer events meet, including the way in which significant adults will be available to help the child grow. Equally important are the child's unique constitutional endowment and the social, cultural, economic, historical and political surroundings. The interaction of inner need, external events and environment will dictate the outcome of the child's adaptation.

Those who work to help children master life stress will need to understand these complex factors and to be aware of some of the normal stresses of development, examples of which follow. These are chosen from the actual productions of children, some of whom were in psychotherapy, others of whom were not.

Each of the illustrations provides the reader with an exercise in thinking developmentally and observing common phase-specific issues in relation to external events and their surrounding circumstances. In addition, the material provides opportunity for speculating about whether the child's responses seem age appropriate or whether they carry the seeds of difficulty.

LOSING A TOOTH

Several themes recur in the following compositions, written by nine- and ten-year-old children as they recall the loss of a first tooth. What is remarkable is how much these children can recapture of the event and the feelings it generated—albeit with some distortion. Parenthetically, this ability to "recapture" is an essential ingredient in the therapeutic process.

Most children lose their first teeth at about age six. Consider, therefore, the developmental processes and the psychosocial, psychosexual forces which converge at that age. Recall that these are written by nine- and ten-year-olds, looking back.

HOW I FELT WHEN I LOST
MY FIRST TOOTH

DONALD
9½ years old

When I lost my tooth I felt like I was going to cry. I felt like taking something away from me. I felt sick, too. Before it was going to come out I was scared.

SUSAN
9 years

One day mother and I went to dress store. One of my teeth came out. I gave my tooth too mother and when we left the store she had lost it, and when I went home I was unpappy very very very sad, and I don't even get to say good-by.

LAURA
10 years

When I lost my first tooth I felt sorry for myself. I felt sorry for myself because it was mines' and it belonged to me. I hated to lose it because I would get nothing for it.

NANCY
10 years old

My first tooth came off a long time ago. Mother was going to pull it off. But I had a feeling it would hurt. So she took me to a dentist.

I was young of age and had never been to a dentist, so I thought it would hurt. But later the dentist spray something that made my tooth stiff for about three minutes. Then he came back and pull it off. It didn't even hurt.

That night I went to bed with my tooth under the pillow. The next morning I had a dime under my pillow. I knew my mother put it there when I slept, not the fairies!

I didn't mind loosing the tooth because it hurt me.

TRACY
10 years old

I didn't feel a thing when my first tooth came out.

But the second tooth really ached. I started to cry because the doctor told me it was out. It was my favorite tooth.

I used it to eat with when I was 3 years old. I didn't have a very good appetite after I came back from the doctors.

Then I got another tooth and I was happy. I said to myself that my third tooth will be as good as the second.

BARBARA
10 years

When I lost my first tooth I used to push my tounge against my tooth. It made a crackling noise. One day I made it very loose. My father told me to open for he had some candy. I'd believed him and when I opened my mouth he stuck his finger in and made a loud crack. That crack scared me. I didn't eat I was scared that crack would soon come again but it hurted so much. But now I still do the crackling noise because that means to pull my tooth so that my father could hear it because I was scared to make a louder crack than his.

LOUIS
10 years

When I was 2 my sister told me that in my body is very important and when I fell I lost my first tooth. When I cried my mother came running in so fast that I thought was a goner. So I felt that the tooth was my life. So when my mom through away the tooth I thought they want me to die. So I went over at garbage to get back my tooth. When I found it I tryed put it back on. Then my sister came through away my tooth and asked me why I want the tooth and I said because I don't want to die. Then she explained that won't die.

Now I think that am rich because I got a mouthful of 25.

SAMUEL
10 years

When I lost my first tooth I felt very funny at first. And when I eat I still felt funny. But then I felt not as funny as I used to because I got use to it. But it really meant a lot to me because it was the tooth I chewed on. Then a few weeks later my gum felt funny. It ache! Another week later I saw a white part on my gum. I asked my mother what it was. She told me it was a baby tooth growing. Then a month went by and the tooth grew to be as the same size as my old one.

Losing a Tooth, in Review

The loss of a tooth raises several important issues. The loss occurs in the mouth, influencing vital functions such as eating and speech. It visibly alters facial appearance, affecting self-perception and how one is perceived by others. Issues of body integrity are central because of these and because of altered sensations within the mouth. Sometimes pain and bleeding are involved. Since the child's cognitive development is immature at age six, it may not be clear that the lost tooth will, in fact, be replaced. The process of replacement, which occurs over time, can be puzzling and potentially magical. This commonplace biological event, even if understood, typically raises further questions about body parts which may be lost, replaced or transformed.

This is the stuff from which fantasies, confusion and mastery emerge. Since the event involves a loss, such fantasies may be related to the child's earlier experiences with loss and separation or bodily injury. Social exchanges with other children—classmates, siblings and others who have already lost teeth or who are currently at the same stage—may influence the individual child's thoughts and feelings about this experience. Family and cultural rituals may have an important impact. The elaborate rituals evolved by different cultures to mark this seemingly minor event testify to its universal significance.

The particular examples demonstrate the various defensive and restitutive atttmpts children use in coping with this event. We see the children make use of dentists and others. The temporary substitute of coins bridges the delay before the real replacement. Some children utilize denial, others turn this passive experience into active coping, while still others displace, substitute and intellectualize.

Donald, like many of the children, shows us his feelings of sadness, and his sense of loss. It is difficult to discern whether this was experienced by Donald as an active or passive loss: "I felt like taking something away from me." "Sick" may refer to the pain or to the loss. Donald also tells us about his anticipatory anxiety. In one brief paragraph, he has given us a mixture of many thoughts and feelings.

Susan quickly associates the event with her mother, upon whom some responsibility is displaced for her double loss. Note the slips of the pen: "too" and "unpappy." She is "very, very, very" sad and presents a sense of the event as happening all too rapidly, perhaps depriving her of the opportunity to mourn for the lost tooth.

Laura again portrays the sadness. Autonomy and body integrity are centrally woven into Laura's account. It is as though Laura experienced the loss as an affront and injustice. She may well be angry and wonders about adequate compensation for something so clearly dear and very much part of her.

Nancy first portrays her efforts to distance the event in time. Secondly, she calls on adults—her mother and the dentist—though each have virtues and liabilities. Again distancing, she remembers that the real experience was not as bad as the painful fantasy, and there is a moment of triumph. Nancy's reflections about the tooth fairy demonstrate the theme of magical replacement and the effort to read reality accurately.

Tracy starts with denial and probably condenses several lost teeth into the story of the second—a different form of displacement. Clearly, this experience has been frightening, and we witness once again an effort to master through distancing. It is as though she were saying: "I couldn't eat as well as in the good old days." Note the generalizing of the difficulty in eating to loss of appetite, followed then by the replacement, with its associated relief and pleasure bolstered by a small sermon to herself.

Barbara begins with a common reaction when a tooth loosens: "I used to push my tongue against my tooth," suggesting her memory of the sensations and her own activity. However, her account from that point on seems somewhat unusual. Sound, an auditory mode, becomes the focus and the vehicle for expressing her general fear and her more specific worry that unless she manages this loss, it will be managed for her by her father. Nevertheless, she remains concerned about outdoing her father, who, in the first instance, tricked her. Despite her special responses, Barbara shares with the other children anxieties about the loss of function, eating and pain, commonly associated with this event. There are suggestive hints in her use of the present tense that this past experience is still not fully integrated.

Louis reaches into the long ago, recalling that his sister had tried to initiate him to the mystery and importance of his body. Yet, knowledge and preparation cannot adequately contain fantasy and anxiety nor offset the actual experience. His fear is total; tooth and life are equated. Though his mother quickly responds, she further "insults" him by disposing of the vital body part, leaving him with the belief that the "helpers" may want him to die. Now, his own creative efforts to retrieve and reattach his tooth (life) take over. Another important female, the sister, appears equally bent on disposal, but finally is able to give in its place the reassuring information. The final substitution which supports Louis is the replacement in coinage. He is now not only intact—but rich.

Samuel immediately goes to the affect, describing his feeling "funny." We are at first unsure whether this feeling is humorous or odd. He confuses past and present as he describes the effect on his eating. His attention is drawn to the past once again in his reference to how it "used to" be as well as the mastery in getting "use to" it. Shifting, Samuel tells us how serviceable and important that tooth was. Shifting once again, he gives a detailed and sequential story of the process of restitution—which, in its changing phases, itself engenders stress. Typically, he uses a significant adult for comfort and finally reaches equilibrium when the new tooth becomes both a substitute and a resurrection.

Morton

The following is an excerpt of an early treatment hour in which a six-year-old, enuretic boy, Morton, gives an account of the loss of a first tooth almost as it occurs, rather than reconstructed from memory. We choose to overlook the treatment issues here in favor of the developmental themes as they are portrayed in the interview.

"As Morton and I entered my office, he proceeded to tell me that he had lost a tooth since our last meeting. It was his very first tooth, and he quickly showed me the hole in the bottom row. I asked when and how it had happened, and he explained that it had happened at night after he had been asleep for awhile. He woke up, wiggled it and finally pulled it out.

Therapist: What did you do then?
Morton: I went and showed it to my mother and dad.
Therapist: What did they say?
Morton: Nothing.
Therapist: Did it hurt or bleed?
Morton: No . . . but it did bleed when I tried to pull it out before. But then it wasn't ready to come out.
Therapist: Did you know before that your teeth would start to come out? Did your mother and dad tell you about it?
Morton: No, they didn't say anything . . . but, you know, all the kids at school had teeth coming out, so I knew from them.

"I commented that he did not know, then, that children of his age lost teeth and grew new ones.

"Morton got out the checkers, as he had done many times during previous hours. We played while the conversation about his tooth continued. He won the game with very little coaching from me. I asked how he felt about winning that day (this is a persistent theme). He said he liked it better than winning the last time.

"He then explored more of the toys. He put on the puppet sheep's-head; but this time, contrary to every other occasion, the puppet did not bite at all. He took the puppet off—moving to the airplane which he had taped up during the previous hour. This time he removed the scotch tape from the plane's windows. He remarked that he remembered putting the tape on, but 'today it looks funny.' Next, he constructed a fishing game in which he used a magnet to fish for paper clips from the wastepaper basket. He asked me to pull the string when he caught 'a fish.' He used a rubber knife to stab each fish as he caught it. After we had played this way for some minutes, Morton asked if I would buy him a second magnet so he could take it home.

"He told me that he hoped his mother would be gone that night so they could eat in a restaurant. I asked what he meant; and he told me that one night a week, his mother goes to school, so daddy takes them out to eat. 'I think tonight might be the night.' He liked going to restaurants because there he could choose his favorite foods."

Discussion

The loss of a tooth is clearly important to Morton. He presents it immediately as he enters the treatment hour, which is replete with metaphoric references to the event. Morton reports that it occurred at night and that he had, in fact, wiggled it out himself. Events which take place at night, in the dark, are often presented by children as a way of acknowledging that they themselves are really "in the dark" and that they do not fully understand what is happening. Morton, like many of the children who wrote about the loss of their first tooth, reveals his wish to manage this body change through activity: *I* made it happen. He calls upon his mother and father to share in the occurrence, but we cannot know from their "nothing" response whether he is disappointed. Perhaps his disclosure that other children prepared him hints at reliance on others rather than his own parents, but it is typical for six-year-olds to begin to alter primary attachments to family members by giving more importance to the world of peers.

There are many metaphoric references to the loss of the tooth and Morton's effort at mastery. In contrast to his prior use of the sheep as a biting animal, the sheep is now restrained. He removes the scotch tape from the plane's window, remarking that today, like his feeling funny about the tooth, the plane appears to look funny. Constructing a fishing game, we see things being connected, through string and magnet; it is as if Morton attempts to control the appearance and disappearance of his "fish." Morton can make the fish disappear and he can retrieve these at will, but he stabs each of the "fish" as if they are somehow offensive—or perhaps frightening. His wish for restitution may be inferred from these activities and from his request to his therapist to provide him with his own second magnet which he will keep with him at home.

The hour ends with his account of eating out and his wish to share something with his father while mother goes about her own affairs. Henry's active efforts at coping with this event, his concern with disappearance and reappearance, his wish to create replacements as well as his efforts to connect to his father are all age appropriate, though their particular manifestations reveal clues to Morton's psychological difficulties as well.

THE BIRTH OF A SIBLING

The birth of a new child has important impact on the structure and dynamics of a family, requiring adjustments and readjustments from all its members. Such an event will have different meanings and will call forth various responses from the children already in the family. Meanings and responses will be shaped by many factors, among which the following are frequently central:

The age and developmental phase of the other child.

The ordinal position of each child in the sibship.

The objective circumstances of the family at the time of the new child's arrival, including its finances, housing, familial supports, the presence or absence of other external stresses, etc.

The psychological circumstances within the family, including especially the adults' receptivity to the new child and their continuing psychological availability to the older children.

The sex of the new sib.

The cognitive and affective preparation of the older children.

The preexisting adaptation, coping style and the maturation of the older children.

It is rare that envy and jealousy will not accompany the "blessed event." At times, these rivalrous feelings have been overstressed; they are, nevertheless, common and frequently appear in indirect and subtle ways, often cloaked in excessive pronouncements of pleasure in and love for the new baby.

The following three illustrations portray different children's reactions to a birth within the family. The responses differ in content and style. One anticipates the birth, another reacts intensely while his mother is in the hospital, and the third child struggles to cope with the recent event, over time.

Diane's Drawings

The following drawings were created by Diane, an unusually

bright, expressive five-and-one-half-year-old girl, shortly before her mother gave birth to a second child. The pregnancy was planned and anticipated with pleasure by both parents, who prepared Diane for the new baby. The drawings were spontaneously created by Diane over a period of several days.

We know that children are often able to express in action many of the conflicts, concerns, ideas and fantasies which they are, for a variety of reasons (including age), unable to state verbally. Drawings present a marvelous "midway" path for such expression because they are neither distinct verbalizations nor actions. Like other play, drawings allow children to express feelings and thoughts in safe terms, permitting some distance from the self and others through displacement.

No inquiry was made about the drawings with Diane. In contrast, when evaluating or treating a child, tactful inquiry can elicit further elaboration of the fantasies and concerns, or "stories" may spontaneously accompany a drawing, giving further clues about the child's inner life. Here, the drawings stand on their own and, consequently, our inferences and interpretations remain tentative, unsupported by Diane's responses.

In reviewing these six drawings together, we can be certain that Diane is an unusually bright, creative and imaginative youngster. She is clearly precocious. Her drawings are unusually well executed figures with considerable detail and clear sex and size differentiation. Her talent is evident in tht whimsy and charm of her drawings, which also suggest that her world is rich in stimulation and exposure to music, art and books. Since the pregnancy themes are so fully portrayed, it is reasonable to infer that there has been much discussion and preparation for the anticipated birth.

Despite this child's precocity, much in the drawings is quite age and phase appropriate. Animals are typically used to represent humans by children of this age in drawings and stories. The persistence of animal stories and fairy tales which have delighted children throughout the ages is testimony to this.

The impending birth can be seen in all the drawings. In some, the rounded figures and their attachments and projections suggest preparation and understanding. Nevertheless, Diane's understanding is, of course, not based on full anatomical and physiological knowledge.

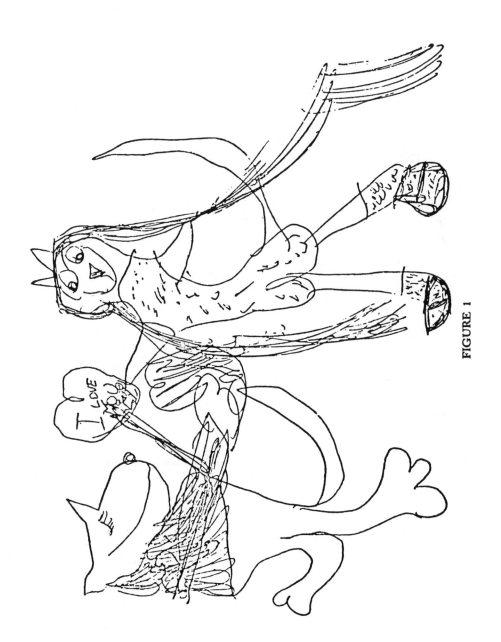

FIGURE 1

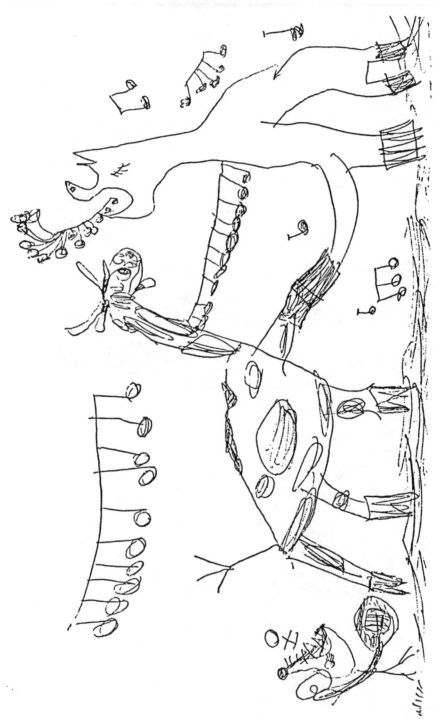

FIGURE 2

FIGURE 3

FIGURE 4

FIGURE 5

FIGURE 6

Where things are contained and where they emerge differs in the drawings. The five- or six-year-old typically has notions about all the body orifices as possible impregnation and birth sites. The mouth and the digestive tract are perhaps the most common areas of misconception. Many of the drawings suggest fragmentary understanding, with confusion and clarity side by side. The mysteries of sexuality for young children cannot be eradicated by the provision of the most thorough information given with the best of intentions. While it is important to provide straightforward information, it is essential that it be age appropriate and that the adult stand prepared to appreciate the child's continuing confusion, as the best information is modified and distorted by the pressures of the particular developmental phase.

In reviewing each drawing, the following observations and inferences suggest themselves:

In Figure 1, two apparently adult figures are represented. One appears to be female and more person-like, the other male and more animal-like. Both have tails—one pointed forward, the other backward. Both smile and are apparently happy together. They are connected in two ways, coming together in the center by an unclear "scribble" and above by a heart-shaped cartoonist balloon containing a verbal message. Interestingly, within this balloon is a repetition of two tiny stick figures. Insides and things-within-things seem important; this interest persists in all the drawings. The fact that the female's eyes are open while the "male" figure's are closed is of interest but remains unclear as to its meaning for Diane.

Figure 2 appears to be a further elaboration of a "romance." This family's interest in music is portrayed, serving to connect the two main figures and perhaps to represent some idea about important things emerging from the mouth. In this drawing, both figures are more animal-like and the sex of each is less clear. However, a few clues suggest that the larger figure on the left, whose insides are more detailed and whose eyes are open, may be the female. Another clue is the proximity of the smaller but much more ambiguous figure to the assumed female adult. Of course, failing the child's validation, these observations are nothing more than hunches.

In contrast to the first drawing, these figures all rest on firm ground, supported by three extremities and connected by a fourth.

Threesomes are represented differently in several of the drawings.

Figure 3, although still whimsical, is the first of a less happy figure. It is hard to be sure whether the lion's face expresses anger, bewilderment, frustration or some mixture of these. The claws and teeth are prominent, while things-within-things appear again in the face within the mane and the planter on the lion's back. Once again, threesomes are represented by the plants growing from it and those which appear to remain inside. The suggested motion of this figure as well as others reveals once again Diane's intelligence and expressive talent. The lion's destination and objective remain unclear, though he seems to be quite purposeful.

Figure 4 depicts a larger female figure and smaller male suggesting either mother and child or older girl and younger boy. They are connected by an unclear projection emanating from the smaller, male figure's groin. This connects with the female's hand and less directly with the round "scribbled" area coming from her mouth. One thinks about umbilical and sexual connections, mindful, again, of the common oral pregnancy notions of young children. Note also the female's pointed thumb and backward glance at a round free floating object behind her. Some attention is drawn to the female's lower half by the heavy lines.

Another couple is shown in Figure 5. Here, the larger is obviously male and the smaller female. The many balloons have other figures connected to the two main characters. Five of these attached to the man's right hand have figures within them, the largest of which is the most confusing. Although the main characters smile at one another, the "balloons" in the left hand of each appear to be slightly doleful animal heads. In contrast to other drawings where the figures are directly connected, these two, while clearly interacting, are not quite touching. The child figure's dress is filled-in and the scalloped hem raises speculative questions about Diane's understanding of sexual anatomy and the physiology of birth.

Figure 6, the last drawing, remains concerned with a couple, although the behavior of the prone figure with the curious body configuration is indecipherable. The girl engages in age-appropriate jump-rope play; the rope itself encloses her. Once again the scalloped hem appears as part of a well detailed dress. It is possible that the line ending with the figure three was a first attempt to draw that arm and hand. However, we note again the importance of "three-ness."

Diane seems well prepared and actively dealing with her thoughts and feelings about the impending birth. Such drawings provide the clinician with a valuable source of understanding about the inner life and developmental tasks of a particular child.

Tommy

The following account describes an intense reaction to the birth of a sister:

Tommy, a seven-year-old boy, was admitted to the pediatric ward with a severe concussion, following a fall from a second story window. His eyes were blackened, and there were many cuts and bruises on his face. When asked what happened, he told the following story:

"Well, my mother went to the hospital to have a baby brother for me, and I was watching for them to come back out of the window; and what I didn't know is that they came in the back door, and my baby brother—he just pushed me out that window."

In fact, the mother was not due from the hospital until the following day. Only the housekeeper was with him at the time Tommy fell, and she was in the kitchen.

In addition to the stress of anticipating the baby, Tommy appears to be suffering from the absence of his mother. The expected distress about this separation may well be compounded by the mother's well-intended "preparation." Tommy may have been less than pleased by such a gift and tells us about his explanation of its causes. It is very possible that Tommy is disturbed by the birth and may need to reverse wishes and fantasies aimed at the new baby, redirecting the aggression against himself. If the baby is a "gift" for him, the common negative reactions associated with sibling births may be more unacceptable and more difficult to express directly. His own guilt and the real or imagined family prohibitions against ambivalence serve to intensify the conflict while reducing Tommy's opportunities to cope more effectively. Tommy's "accident" may have been his only unconscious option in attempting to manage his dilemma.

Tommy's response to a normative event is sufficiently serious to warrant further evaluation and further psychotherapeutic assistance. Timely intervention in such instances can help to relieve psychological difficulty. Close collaboration between pediatric-ward staff and child psychiatric personnel permits rapid identification and prompt intervention on behalf of such children.

David

The following is a summary of a series of observations presented by a highly sophisticated observer about a child's behavior prior to and following the birth of his sister.

David, an only child, was two years and four months old when his sister was born. He made it clear to his parents that he understood that a new baby was on the way. When his mother was six months pregnant, David reacted to a comment about baby-sitting arrangements one evening by saying, "I know, Mommy. The baby is in there," pointing to her protruding abdomen.

David's parents prepared him for the birth in various ways: They talked about the new baby; they showed him the new baby's room; they showed him pictures of babies; and he had seen friends with babies. Whenever he brought up questions about the forthcoming arrival, they openly discussed his interest or concerns. Neither the exact anatomical details of birth nor the baby's precise internal location was particularly stressed, but it was clear that David knew that the baby was "in there."

From his bedroom window, David enjoyed watching the cars passing below on a busy city street. Many of his first words had to do with cars. He was very good at identifying them: "That is a car like Daddy's" (or like Mummy's or like Granpa's). Soon after he became aware of the fact that his mother was pregnant, he also became very interested in garages. He would build garages and ask his mommy or daddy to build them. He would spend much time putting the cars in the garages and taking them out. His grandfather had a garage whose door opened and closed and when David visited, he continually lifted the door up and down to make sure the car was inside. David talked about the car's being asleep: "It is going night-night." He liked to run around to the back of the garage and look into the window to see that the car was still there even when the door was down.

As his mother's pregnancy progressed, his interest in garages—especially garages with doors which opened and closed—increased. When his mother was nearly at term, David would use her body as a "garage." He would park cars between her breasts and abdomen and talk about that place as being a driveway or a garage. During the last two months of her pregnancy, David's favorite toy was a house which had a garage that opened and closed.

David had been told that his mother would go to the hospital to have his new baby brother or sister. Since he was unfamiliar with hospitals, this did not particularly distress him; however, he was concerned about her visiting the doctor because of his own mild apprehensions about his experience with doctors. When his mother entered the hospital, his anxiety increased—particularly since he remembered that the trip had something to do with doctors. Speaking to her on the telephone, however, relieved some of his anxiety.

On one occasion during his mother's hospitalization David, his father and his maternal grandmother went to a restaurant. The waitress asked about his mother. His first reply was that she was "at the doctor's making a baby." Then he said that she was not at the doctor's but at the *hospital* and had, in fact, already made his new sister. He repeated the words, "baby" and "sister" several times.

His mother remained in the hospital for three days. During this time, his maternal grandmother, his father and a live-in student were at home with David. He seemed slightly concerned as to the whereabouts of his mother, but the presence of other people seemed to "tide him over" quite well.

David's parents planned their strategy for his mother's return home with great care. Mother would step from the car with the baby in her arms, and when David approached, she would pivot, hand the baby to the father and hug David to reassure him of her interest. When the moment actually arrived, David was not at all interested in the new baby. He gave it a cursory glance and quickly took mother off to show her the various flowers which he and his grandmother had planted in the garden. When they entered the house David regaled his mother with stories about the activities he had enjoyed while she was gone. After some time he approached the baby and studied her for a few minutes. He returned to his mother and looked somewhat perplexed. "That's the new baby?" he asked. His mother assured him that it was. "But, where is the baby's Mommy?"

His mother explained that she was Jessica's mommy *and* David's mommy, too. He continued to insist his mommy was *his* mommy and *not* the baby's.

For several days afterward the word "my" appeared more frequently in David's vocabulary. Objects were usually prefaced with the word "mine." In addition his hand trembled quite noticeably when he patted the infant. He was interested in patting quite firmly and sometimes he squeezed the baby too hard. On the other hand, David attempted to play the part of "big brother." However, while he was helpful to his mother and others around the house, he found it difficult to control both his aggressiveness and his own dependency needs. If there were a lot of people around—especially a lot of children—he became highly excited and rambunctious. When overtired, he behaved similarly.

David made it very clear that he resented the attention which the new baby received. On one occasion when visitors asked about Jessica, David informed them that she was upstairs sleeping when, in fact, the baby was in the same room.

Four days after the baby's arrival, David watched the preparation of a turkey for dinner. "What is that?" he said, pointing to the opening in the turkey.

"What do you think it is?" his father asked.

"I know what it is. . . . It's a garage."

"A garage?"

"Yes," David assured him. "That's where the cars go and can be parked."

Ten days later, David seemed to be adjusting. Although still interested in cars and garages, he no longer used his mother as a parking lot.

Discussion

David's responses to his sister's birth are typical for a bright and well-prepared two-and-one-half-year-old. Remembering his own experiences, David portrays his appropriate concern for his mother's safety and temporary unavailability. Adult permission to play out his concerns helps him master an event which he can only partially understand. He is also permitted to demonstrate increased tension and irritability when the baby actually arrives and to retain the quite age-appropriate stance of "the world revolves around me."

He is accorded the right to express verbally and behaviorally that he is less than totally pleased with the new arrival. Using play, ideas he can grasp, important people for comfort and constancy when he is confused, David is helped to manage this stress.

GOING TO CAMP

The first time away from home typically creates anxiety for children. Camp, pleasurable as it may be, requires more independent functioning, meeting new people, managing unfamiliar routines, tolerating new foods and regulation by different and, at first, unknown adults. Often, children are prepared for this experience through a litany of the many joys to come. While reassuring, the presentation of only the positive can lead a child to believe that homesickness or anticipatory anxiety is childish, unacceptable and unusual. Thus, they imagine that such feelings are unique, further increasing the stress and anxiety. Most children manage camp with reasonable equanimity depending upon age, the length of time away from home, previous separations and preparation for this event, and permission to express the pleasure and anxiety this experience can generate. It is important to note that, once mastered, the event can become central to the child's progression, teaching him to know that a feared event lies within his management and expands his self-reliance.

The following two letters were sent by children during their first camp stay.

Albert

> *DEAR MOMMY AND*
> *DADDY*
>
> *I wish you would send me the sports section of the Chron-*

icle every day. It think it would be very nice of you if you took me out of this stupid camp. I have four reasons I would like to get out of here they are:

1. Grusome Grossman
2. Sammy Sucker
3. Prune Garder
4. Sweetyboy

and I just rememered my five they call me Rosenlick, last but not least its a lousy camp. But I want to thank both of you for surprising me with those baseball books and the other book. I wish I could get out of this place. Say hello to Nonny for me and to Nicky when he returns. This was written to you on the first Monday I was here.

Love, Albert

Albert portrays his homesickness and age-appropriate efforts to cope with his first lengthy separation from home.

Alluding to the disruption of his daily routines, he reaches for the missed and the familiar at home. He associates this directly to homesickness, labeling the camp with a typical nine-year-old's invective: "stupid." With forthright, logical listing—a useful defensive ordering —he points to four reasons for wanting to return home. The play on words which label and identify suggests that he is actively doing to others what he has himself experienced as unpleasant—being called a funny name. In any case, he says directly that it is a lousy camp—suggesting that Albert is permitted to convey such attitudes at home.

Now the letter begins to sound conventional, thanking his parents for sending books he prizes, while he sends regards to others at home. These typical sentences provide connections to familiar people and things. However, his homesickness and plea for rescue surface in the midst of these comments.

It is possible that the last sentence was added some time later and suggests that his distress is already diminished.

Marc

tuesday

DEAR ALL,

Outdoor Ed is a lot of fun, but I'm extreamly homesick, and aside from that I feel plain nautious. M.r.s. A is going to drive down for a meeting tomorrow, and I don't know whether or not to stay. It is okay when I'm doing somthing. But I always wake up during the night and tremble and it feels like I'm going to vomit. I'm sorry about the bad news, so I'll tell you some good news. Uncle Waldo played the old multiplying letter trick on me. But I caught a cabin leader at it. I was the first to see the apple in the apple game. I will call you so we can make a decision. I really feel miserable But the schedule looks so fun, excpect a call.

Love, Marc

Marc, 11, is away from home for the first time. His letter portrays his struggle with a conflict that is all too plain to him.

It is fun, yet. . . . His homesickness is experienced fully and Marc knows clearly that his "nautious," gut reactions are related to his not knowing whether to stay. This sensitive, articulate boy understands how activity mutes the conflict, while the night, being alone and "at rest" intensifies it. While he is alert to the possible disappointment this might create for "all" he clearly can rely on his family for their understanding, preparing them for consultation in his decision. His "good news"—which he wants to convey to his family—involves his ability to understand a game before other children. Temporarily, this mastery serves to bolster his sense of self-esteem which has been shaken by his conflict, but it is only temporary solace for he really feels "miserable." He longs to stay but he also understands the limits of his own capacity. This is an unusual degree of self-awareness for an 11-year-old, a capacity which ironically sharpens Marc's conflict.

We are left to "excpect a call."

HOSPITALIZATION

Clearly the hospitalization of a child creates stress for the child and his family. Once again, the child's reaction will depend on many personal and familial factors as well as his age and developmental stage. The specific illness, treatment procedures and the routines of the pediatric ward will also color the child's experience and reactions to the hospitalization. For example, for one child, the critical issue may be separation from his family; for another, fear of body damage may assume greater significance.

There is a large body of excellent literature describing the variations of childhood reaction to the hospital and its procedures. It is not our intent to restate this material in detail. However, the following considerations are important in the understanding of any child's way of organizing and responding to the experience. These include separation, pain, anxiety about real or imagined body injury and alterations in perception, such as those accompanying toxicity and immobilization.

The enforced passivity, often necessary, can create or intensify regressive pulls. The environment of the hospital is peculiar. Space, furniture, medical equipment, daily routines and people are all unfamiliar, creating a completely new ecology for the child and his family. Even a familiar object, like a bed, is different in a hospital. Treatment procedures are often mysterious and painful. Commonly, children have great difficulty in understanding how such procedures can benefit them. It is not unusual for bewilderment and rage to be directed against parents for their seeming failure to protect. In the usual routine of pediatric care, many procedures are carried out when the child feels well, creating even greater mystification.

The Walking Pneumonia Tapes

The following notes are sections from the verbatim, tape-recorded comments of a 14-year-old boy, who was hospitalized for six days as the result of a respiratory infection. The boy's therapist suggested making these recordings in order to help the patient cope with this stressful experience. To assist the reader, we have provided a running commentary of some of these issues side by side with the account itself.

Account

They said they were putting me in the adolescent ward, and I get up here and I'm surrounded by babies—and do they yell! The only other adolescent is a girl, and she is at the other end of the ward, and I walked down there and that big nurse yelled like I was going to rape her or something. I mean the girl, not the nurse. That nurse scares me I think she *enjoys* giving shots in the ass. Anyhow, that girl had her appendix out, so she's not swinging any, but she still looks pretty sexy in that nightgown. I'm gonna get her phone number and then maybe we can compare scars or something. . . .

. . . That big nurse came in again, and she tells me I have to pee in a can and they're going to *save* it! Did you ever try to pee in one of those things? It's cold as hell and you have to stick it in there, because otherwise you might miss; and if you spill some, God only knows what would happen, because they're saving the stuff and you might throw the whole laboratory out of kilter. I wonder if they think I might have syphilis or something. You'll have to tell me, Dr. B., what saving pee has to do with pneumonia! Anyhow, what I started to say is that this big nurse is telling me about the pee-

Commentary

He's displaced—and even worse, he's been tricked. Babies yell— a possible hint of regressive pulls. Efforts to find a friend are thwarted by the nurse who becomes the enemy. The humor and precocity are protective and run through the entire material.

Procedures are mysterious and lead to alternating feelings of helplessness and omnipotence. What secrets will they learn and keep from him? Are they on to his sexual interests, and have these caused his trouble? Humiliation about his exposure is heightened by the nurse's casual and unintended seductive remark.

ing jar, and she says I have beautiful eyes. It really throws me. You know who tells me I have beautiful eyes? Queers and batty old ladies on the bus. . . . If any girl I know ever told me I have beautiful eyes, I would think she was a nut. Somebody ought to tell some of these nurses how to talk to teenagers. . . .

. . . I couldn't sleep that first night. I don't think I was scared or anything like that, but I didn't want to stay in that big room by myself. And that kid who was hit by a car was yelling for his mother something awful. Anyhow, I sat up and talked to that nice night nurse. She is the best one and she let me have a cigarette. And I held her knitting for her. You'd think I was a nut, sitting there knitting at four o'clock in the morning. If the guys ever found that out, I'd be ruined. . . .

. . . They won't let me smoke. They tell me it is too bad about the rule, but you can only smoke in the waiting room. Then they tell me that since I have a private room, I can't go out to the waiting room to start with. I told them that was not very smart thinking, that it didn't even *sound* right, but a rule is a rule, they say. So I have to sit on my private john to

At night, and in the quiet, the fears are more clear, but quickly denied. He finds an ally, thus permitting some acceptable passivity and intimacy. But who will find out?

Catch 22—hospitals are full of them. Yet, the anxiety about not conforming to mystifying rules is expressed. The way out is to become more grown up—but at what price?

smoke, and I don't even like to smoke that way. Besides, I'm afraid I might forget myself and lose some pee. I think you better get me out of this place and put me in with the adults, even if they have diseases or dreadful things. If this is an adolescent ward, you can have it—except for that night nurse. . . .

. . . Right after I woke up this morning and had my bath—and, believe me, I'd rather smell than be *washed;* it's too embarrassing. . . . But I'll have to talk with you about that. . . . Anyhow, the door bursts open, and in comes this Father talking like crazy and waving his hands and blessing everybody in the place and some who aren't even in the place, I think. And he asked me where I go to school, and I knew I was ruined because I had to say St. John's. He gets really excited then and pulls out his beads and says I have to give him a confession. So what could I do? I haven't given them any confessions in years, but this nut —and he *is* a nut—has me trapped in my pajamas waving them beads around dangerously. So I give him a confession. Like I say, I don't mind my mother and I cheated once in a school; and it is all my fault, I have something called the walking pneumonia, because I went surfing

A simple routine becomes an affront and an invasion of privacy. Enter another character—strange but familiar and certainly unwanted. He is trapped into compliance—exposure is again an issue, and the best he can do is to compromise with his integrity. Fears emerge and flight looks better and better.

when it was freezing. I didn't give him any of that stuff about girls or sex or anything, because this guy was wild enough to start with. He blessed me all over the place and said I would do better when the pneumonia stopped walking. That would probably mean I was dead or something. And he left, saying he would come to see me every day. I gotta get out of this place. You asked if I needed anything. What about a rope and a pair of pants?

. . . I was changing my pajamas and the door burst open, and this very strange old lady came running in. And there I was, bareassed, and she says, "Little boy, I have something for you!" Well, I quick jumped behind the bed just in case, and she said she had a puppet to give me. I said, "*A what?*" And she said, "A happy puppet from the volunteers!" I thought for a minute that maybe the soldiers were making something for us. So I told her she should take the puppet to one of those little kids who's always yelling, but she wouldn't even listen. She says she has hundreds of puppets and all the boys and girls get one, and they even get one for every week they stay. And I say, "What will I do with a puppet? I'm 14-years-old." But nothing

Intrusions never stop. He can't regulate their comings and goings, nor the invasions of his privacy. He does manage to control himself, again through humor, but he's getting increasingly desperate to maintain a grown-up posture.

stops her, so I have this stupid-looking puppet. I hope she doesn't ever decide to give away a disease. There would be an epidemic. I'm behaving myself though. I didn't tell her what she could do with the puppet. I think you'd better forget about the rope. Just bring me some pants, and I will really have the walking pneumonia.

. . . She even gave a puppet to that kid whose arms are all casted. . . .

In one sentence, he captures the absurdity of well meaning but undifferentiated hospital practices.

. . . You know, I can't dream in the hospital. I always have those dreams at home that we talk about; but here it is zero. That's funny when you think of it, since I think this place should give anyone nightmares. . . .

He discovers something interesting about himself and wonders about it. His reflections suggest that characteristic defenses are disrupted under the impact of this strange and worrisome place. Emergency repressions are often necessary in the face of intense stress.

. . . There's something funny about you up here. I always see you in the office, and you sit there and we talk; and I suddenly think I don't know anything about you. I don't even know what kind of car you drive or if you're married or if you have kids. I just know you're not like Dr. Smith was, that you stay at the hospital. But here you're coming up to the ward, and I guess you come

Once again a familiar person is seen differently. As he observes the therapist in a new way, these observations lead him to consider new questions. This may well be an illustration of how a stressful event can create an opportunity for openness and potential progress. His account of the "little kid with the red hair" permits the expression of his own love and need—safely displaced to another. He seems to every day, because you see all the other kids and they know you. In fact, that little kid with the red hair who was in the automobile accident that you're helping to learn to walk *loves* you. They even get him to *eat* by telling him you're coming. I never really thought of you being like a human, you know. If anyone asks me about my doctor, I'm going to tell them it's you. What do you come up here for if none of these other kids are your patients? I guess there is a lot you don't know about me, too; but you sure know a helluva lot more about me than I know about you. You even gave those tests, those crazy inkblots, so you probably even know if I'm going to flip. I know I'm going to flip if I don't get out of here. I'm beginning to feel like that time before, when we talked about when I took the cast off my leg. . . .

. . . After I saw you yesterday, I suddenly decided to call my father; and it's unbelievable: He was *nice*. I didn't even swear at him and he said he would come right over and what could he bring me. So I told him to pick something out. And then I was in a mess, because if he comes and my mother comes, she will crap; so I called her and told her he was coming. Then I wished

be very proud that Dr. B. is his —and very special. His realization that there is much he does not know leads him to the memory of another anxious time— the psychological tests, and a prior inquiry. It all seems put together as the question: From all you know of me, will I be all right?

In his search for help, he risks calling upon his father, whose reliability is doubtful. To his surprise, the gamble works, though it requires self-control and the management of the problem it creates with his mother. This active process is typical of the adolescent's struggle with partial identifications and conflicting loyalties. It works so well that he playfully wonders

I hadn't told her, but I know it would be murder if I didn't. I will remember what you said when we talked about my loving him and hating him at the same time. Maybe I should have asked him for a Honda. . . .

. . . Thanks for bringing me that book and the puzzle. It only took me 20 minutes to figure it out, but 20 minutes in this place is wonderful. The doctor says I can go Saturday, but two more days of this and they will have to lock me up in the padded cell. Are there really padded cells? That big nurse says I am hyperactive. I thought it was something bad, but I think it means that I'm a swinger. I'll be swinging from the ceiling, that's what. Honest, all there is to do is watch TV in the daytime. It's all about doctors and people with strange diseases and operations and dying; so I'm lying here in a hospital looking at that crap, and I begin to think that I'm gonna get something like that, and I think I have a brain tumor because I have those headaches. You'd think the hospital would put in its own TV. Something cheerful or sexy—but not this medical stuff with the blood running out of the tube. . . .

. . . This is a terrible day. Mary, the girl with the appendix—I

whether he should have raised the ante.

Time moves slowly in an environment which enforces passivity and evokes preoccupation with damage and even death. In another place, television might offer some respite; here, every fragment of experience gets contaminated with danger.

This is indeed a terrible day. He is disappointed and aban-

mean without the appendix—
went home. I am the only teen-
ager up here, and everybody else
is a kid or a baby or is dying
or something. And then Dr. T.
came and said I had to stay until
Sunday, and I nearly cried. And
I knew you wouldn't be here
before I went. I just did 20 push-
ups and practically fainted. That
would shake them up—if they
came in and found me passed
out on the floor. I think I am
weak. I will exercise every day.
One of the things I am weak
with is hunger. The food here
is awful. I called my mother
and told her to bring me a dozen
cream puffs, and she said she
would come early, because I
can't go home until tomorrow.
I am going to sit up all night
and roll the yarn for that night
nurse. She is really *great*, Dr. B.
She knows how to *talk* so it
makes sense. Like she told me
about how Greg had to learn to
walk again because his brain got
hurt in the accident. I hope nothing ever happens to my head,
but it is good to know you can
get cured from it. . . .

doned by a peer and his therapist, leaving him even more
frightened and vulnerable to regression. To counter this, he must
become more active and prove
that his body can work. The
effort to prove this causes more
worry. Since nothing seems to
be an effective reassurance, he
must rely on mother as feeder
and upon his friend, the nurse
with whom he can manage the
night.

. . . Do you know they bought
me a lamp for the bed this morning? I've been here six days and
I'm going home, so they bring
me a lamp. "Ha!" I said, "I am
already half-blind in both eyes

Catch 22, Part 2—but he is going home, and he can joke about
it and turn his attention to the
pleasures of freedom. All that
the hospital has denied—privacy,
autonomy, control of others—

from trying to look at things in the dark." So when they found I was going, they took the lamp away. I am going home and smoke a whole package of cigarettes and maybe a cigar if I can get one, and I'm going to take a *bath*. I'm going to take a bath for *two* hours, and if anyone else wants in the bathroom, they'll have to use the Shell station at the corner. . . .

. . . They're going to spring me out of this place. I'm gonna leave the book of facts and the puzzle, and I remembered the 15 cents I owed you from last month and the tape for you to pick up with the nurse. I am going to write a letter to that night nurse, because she gave me her address and said she would answer. . . .

. . . I'll see you Thursday at the same time. The doctor said not to go back to school until Wednesday. And I can't do my paper route for another week and not then if it is raining. Do you know how much *money* I've *lost*? I am not only weak but poor. . . .

. . . You didn't think I'd make it, did you? This is Batman signing off.

grown-upness—is just around the corner.

He begins the process of leaving and settling accounts. He is obviously so glad to leave that he becomes philanthropic. He will leave as much as he can behind, but he will take the night nurse and his therapist with him.

In contrast to the fantasies of freedom in the paragraph above, here he picks up the continuity of his life and more realistically addresses the immediate future. He vividly states his sense of the truly high cost of hospitalization.

This account testifies to the power of the hospital as an all encompassing experience. Few environments can match it for its intensity, intrusiveness and capacity for affecting every detail of daily living.

Matthew

Figure 7 was produced by an eight-year-old boy who was hospitalized for a tonsillectomy and a circumcision. Unfortunately, there were postoperative complications, requiring a second hospitalization during which time he became withdrawn and sporadically enuretic. Work with the child to help him master this obvious trauma began shortly after the second hospitalization. Eight weeks into the psychotherapy, Matthew drew the following Figure 7 and was able to elaborate ón his picture verbally.

Eight weeks after the event, the hospital experience and its personnel are portrayed as fearsome by the child. This is clear from Matthew's representation of a nurse, often the person who is intimately involved in the child's care and who must, on occasion, do painful things as part of the medical treatment. While the drawing is well organized and detailed for an eight-year-old, the overall impact of the figure is formidable. The nurse's mouth is filled with fangs and she has "weapons" in both hands, which are larger than life-size. The hypodermic syringe is held like a dagger, suggesting the common perception and fear of shots. The other instrument is less clear; it may be an ice pack, an enema bag or even a stethoscope —but whatever it is, it is held ready for use. The skirt is elongated and prominent. The nurse's mouth and the odd lower part of her dress may be references to those body parts which were injured in the service of repair.

Matthew's ability to employ some humor in trying to master this event was suggested by his comment about the turned out position of the feet: "It's hard to walk that way." This comment helped Matthew further explore his feelings about the menacing caretakers and his wish to keep them at bay.

Donald

The following are four drawings made by a bright nine-year-old boy who was hospitalized for the removal of a small cyst in his neck.

Figure 8 was drawn on the evening of the day in which the surgery was performed, Figure 9 early the following day, and Figures 10 and 11 on each of the remaining two days in the hospital.

NURSE

FIGURE 7

Donald is an only child of rather anxious parents. His Jewish mother survived the Nazi era. Donald had been hospitalized before on several occasions between the ages of two months and four years—all for rather minor ailments. During his hospitalization his mother remained with him almost constantly, being alternately protective and critical of Donald. She did, however, allow one of the psychiatric social workers who routinely worked on the pediatric ward to talk and play with her son.

Figure 8 vividly conveys Donald's sense of confusion, precariousness and danger. There is a frantic quality to his drawing, with many characters, much action and lots of dialogue. Hospital equipment and surgical paraphernalia are in evidence: the wheelchair, nurses' station, huge dagger (scalpel?), the rotating fans or lights all suggest a kaleidoscopic mixture of the very hectic and confusing surgical experience. Body parts are somewhat misplaced, while the stream of lines coming from the main figure suggests considerable bleeding. His resistance to the surgery is broadcast loudly, while various injunctions and cries for help are directly expressed.

Fragments from the boy's reality are also suggested in the "sorry, no money" and "I not a watter (sic)" since we know that this family was preoccupied by their financial difficulties and an argument had taken place between Donald and his mother earlier that day about whether he wanted a drink of water.

The second drawing (Figure 9) is even more chaotic than the first—suggesting that the disorganizing effect of the experience is still intense. This is not unusual for children who have recently undergone surgery. Despite the chaos, the content has moved away from the hospital directly and toward more general themes of destruction and aggression. Again, body parts are scattered about; however, this time they are totally disconnected. American and German soldiers are in fierce combat, with a ferocious looking German seeming to stand above a supine and fragmented figure labeled "chief." In all the confusion, however, there are elements of beginning order seen in the tic-tac-toe like design—a game that Donald played frequently during the hospital stay.

Figure 10 is, in the main, a well organized Superman figure— appropriate to a child's need to call upon powerful magic to manage

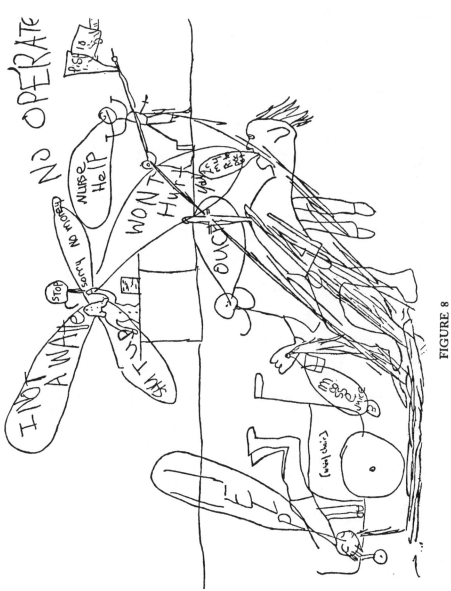

FIGURE 8

FIGURE 9

FIGURE 10

FIGURE 11

intense stress. The figure is well muscled and armed, has both wings and "rockets" on his boots and is seemingly well prepared for fight or flight. He can surely overcome.

Again typical of the recovery process, the fourth drawing (Figure 11) moves further away from the hospital experience, and the human figure is now displaced upon a powerful bird. However, the destructive theme continues in the moving rocket or bomb. It is possible that the "bird" is reaching towards control of the destructive forces or that these forces have barely escaped the bird itself. Either interpretation suggests increasing mastery for Donald.

Viewing the drawings in sequence over the four days of the hospitalization provides us with a vivid illustration of the disruptive impact of surgery and hospitalization and the process of reintegration and recovery.

SLEEPING IN THE DARK

In the prior material, we have discussed children's responses to particular stressful events in development. In this section, the stress is not a new event which has a demarcated beginning or end. Rather, it is a change in reaction to a common experience.

Going to sleep in the dark is a daily occurrence, which is typically not experienced as uncomfortable during certain periods of development. At earlier periods, there may be sleep disturbances and evidence of more diffuse forms of anxiety, but, characteristically, the dark seems to become frightening in a new way sometime after two and most commonly around three. Often, these fears recur in transient forms into a child's latency and beyond. Therefore, it becomes important to ask how such a mundane experience becomes disquieting during a particular developmental period and what prompts this shift. With increasing maturation, the child's experience of nighttime anxiety becomes more organized and focused. This process suggests that the inner life of the child is changing. One element of the change relates to new inner pressures which are mandated by the developmental timetable and which revolve around the child's increasing initiative and self-assertion, and the consequent establishment of a new dynamic interaction with the outer world. A second element of this change is an enhanced capacity for fantasy formation which can be represented as conscious thoughts and images. Of particular importance is the child's capacity to more firmly differentiate the self from the outer world. These shifts create for the child the need and the ability to represent portions of inner conflict as external concerns. Sufficient ego development on a cognitive, affective, interpersonal and defensive level is necessary before the dark can be experienced and communicated in this new, frightening and particular way.

The external circumstances—going to sleep, separating from others, decreasing activity—set the stage for various internal phenomena. The dark itself creates a diminished sensory input, prompting the upsurge of internal impulses and fantasies. Being alone or separated from adult supports may also turn the child's attention inward. Going to sleep requires the yielding of active interchange with people and things, while the relaxation of alertness involves the gradual loss of control and consciousness. Despite the fact that for many children anxiety about the dark may not be triggered by a specific external event, this concern is similar to stress experiences in that it is determined by the interplay between changing inner forces, emerging new capacities and the environment.

In the following section, eight normal children between the ages of five and six respond to the question: *"Do you sleep with the light on?"* Their tape recorded responses follow. Although it is not known if they were asked about fears directly, almost all the children discuss these. They tell us how common such fears are and demonstrate familiar but important efforts at mastery. A clear sense of the uniqueness of each child also emerges from these very brief responses.

> John: *I do sometimes. But I'm not afraid unless the door is closed. Then I'm 'fraid someone bad might come out from under my bed. Once in the country a big bear was under my bed, but he didn't do anything to me. I don't get afraid of bears because they can get dead, but I get afraid of ghosts because they don't get dead.*

John's use of the word "sometimes" in his opening sentence immediately presents a differentiated sense of the world. This "sometimes" not only appears to respond to the question that is asked, but is responsive as well to the question which John frames himself: "Are you afraid?" He answers this question with a qualified negative assertion: "I'm not afraid unless. . . ." John reports that it takes a particular circumstance (the door closed) to evoke fears which are then projected onto "someone bad" and threatening. Sorting these fears, he suggests that "real" objects are less worrisome and mystifying, since they are mortal and more manageable. Ghosts, however, remain to terrify.

> Erica: *If we promise to be quiet, then we get it turned on as a treat. The dark isn't the same all the time. If I've been playing in the dark, I know what it is. But if you've been in the light and go into the dark, you're scared. You kind of dream that a witch is going to come out of the closet.*

Erica suggests that she and a sibling can bargain for greater safety by promising to be good. The manner in which Erica goes on to portray her ability to discern different qualities about the dark is almost poetic. The sense of active mastery when playing in the dark is clearly not the same as moving from one state to another—from light to dark. This may, as well, represent moving from wakefulness to sleep and from active to passive, under one's own direction as opposed to expected behavior. It may also represent "moving" from being in the dark voluntarily as contrasted to being sent there by another. Her summary sentence suggests that only when the dark is not in her control does she become vulnerable to the fears which are typically represented in the form of a frightening witch, who may emerge from a hidden place and take one unawares. But this fear is a "kind of dream," suggesting that Erica has some awareness than the fears are internal. Dream and reality are distinguishable, but at age six, only "kind of."

> Joan: *No! I'm not scared of the dark at all. But I have a little bit of light because mother likes to leave my door open with the hall light on. And I like a little light so when I wake up I can see where I am.*

Joan firmly declares in the negative, clearly suggesting that she is answering both the spoken and the implicit question. Our suspicion that Joan protests too much is confirmed in her comment that it is her mother who wishes that she have a "little light." Joan can reveal her greater comfort when some light is present, yet she must insistently deny the presence of fear in the dark. For Joan, the comfort of the light is focused on its usefulness in being oriented to place.

> Jerry: *No! I don't want it on, and my brother doesn't, either. When I was a baby, I was afraid of the dark. But that was about six years ago. And my brother didn't used to like to stay in the dark, either. He thought a ghost might come in.*

Jerry also firmly declares the bravado which he and his brother share. He displaces any sense of fear onto the very long ago, when such fears would be more acceptable. This displacement is shared once again with Jerry's brother who, however, becomes the spokesman for the fear in its concrete form: the ghost.

> Ann: *I sleep with it off. That's the only way I can get to sleep. And I like the dark because I can pretend then about the Beauty and the Beast. That's a fairy tale we have and I pretend that I'm the Beauty and my sister is the Beast.*

Ann does not protest; she avows that the dark helps her to sleep. There is no direct mention of fear in her response. But there is a description of fantasy. Her use of universal fantasy—a folk tale—allows her to be certain that her thoughts are "pretend."

> Larry: *I like to sleep in the dark because it's funner. I pretend I'm scared to fool my brother. I tell him a monster's in the room and he runs to Mom and says a monster's in the room. Then she turns the light on and she's surprised and he's surprised, and I fooled them.*

Larry initially avows that sleeping in the dark is itself fun although the fun he describes is not sleeping at all. With good humor he describes a trick which he plays on his brother and mother. The trick is simple, yet it serves Larry in many ways: He is not the fearful one, any fear is displaced upon his brother; the fantasied monster which is Larry's invention is now given to his brother leaving Larry with enjoyable affects rather than scary ones; the active trickery serves to ward off fear even further by adding an additional dimension of delight—brother rather than Larry calls upon mother. Perhaps this insures that any shame over Larry's wish for his mother is avoided. The dark is displaced with Larry several steps removed from the wish for the light. Instead, he is the creator of a trick which everyone enjoys.

> Tim: *No, because I don't want anybody disturbing me. If the light is on, people come in to see if I'm all right. Some kids want it on because they want to stay up as late as grownups and they think they're awake just because the light is on. That's kind of silly.*

Tim's response is perhaps the most idiosyncratic. He appears to have put all fear behind him. At age five Tim's response seems to have a remarkably adult "no-nonsense" quality. He does not wish to be disturbed and believes he will be if the light is on. He also philosophizes on the silly notion some kids have about wanting to remain in contact with grownups and imagining that they are awake just because the light is on. His disdain of this childish idea suggests that he has long since outgrown such needs. There is a tiny hint that all is not yet so settled in his comment that people might come in "to see if I'm all right."

> Cynthia: *I sleep better in the dark because the light shines in your eyes too much. But if the hall light isn't on, I'm a little bit afraid. It might look like witches are peeking out of my closet. And don't you know that witches hurt you? Well, they cook you; and that doesn't sound very good to me.*

Cynthia is well aware that the dark may be frightening. Too much light will interfere with sleep but total darkness makes it impossible to feel that she is safe. Without some light by which to recognize the reality of familiar objects, the closet may become a hiding place for dangerous witches. Her differentiation between some light and no light and her use of the phrase "a little bit afraid" may be Cynthia's metaphor for the transitional state between wakefulness and sleep when frightening fantasies may occur. The next phase: "It might look like" is a clue to Cynthia's ability for considerable discrimination, suggesting her capacity—still evolving—to distinguish reality from imagination. This is typical for five-year-olds. Naming the enemy and the enemy action—witches and being cooked—helps to manage her anxiety. There is a suggestion of humor in her summation: "that doesn't sound very good to me."

While there are many common themes in these responses, each child responds in a highly individualized style. In addition to the psychological issues discussed at the beginning of this section, the material demonstrates the following common themes.

1) The use of others for managing anxiety by sharing and/or displacing it. Siblings are helpful in this process in a different but no less important way than parents.

2) The use of fairy tales and figures from folk lore as an ongoing framework for personal fantasy. This reminds us that these universal stories can be useful as well as provocative. The girls speak of witches while the boys speak of ghosts and monsters, suggesting considerable sex differentiation in this very small sample. The data do not give us any way of determining the weight of innate and/or cultural forces in shaping these differences.

3) The use of humor and playfulness as ways of diffusing anxiety.

Each brief response contains an amazing richness in thought, fantasy, feeling, relationship, defensive organization, capacity for fine differentiation and a clear sense of the uniqueness of each child.

MENARCHE

While menarche is a developmental event with a clear onset, body changes typically occur in advance of the first menstrual period.

Most girls have already experienced a spurt in growth, changes in skin texture and the beginning of secondary sexual characteristics, stirring up many new attitudes and feelings. Menarche adds significantly to this process. The emotional state is complex and leads to many contradictory feelings, which may include pleasant, confusing, exciting, mysterious, worrisome and embarrassing affects. Which of these are most prominent for a particular girl will depend upon many physical, cognitive and attitudinal factors.

The health and prior adequacy of body functions will influence the girl's response to menarche. Children who have had a minimum of physical difficulties and who experience their bodies as reliable and competent will tend to be less anxious about menstruating.

Nevertheless, bleeding is commonly connected with injury and the first glimpse of menstrual blood may lead to this association. Even the best prepared girl is likely to experience some shock and concern. Genital bleeding creates a dilemma. The natural impulse to display bleeding and seek help is complicated by social-familial prohibitions about exposing private body parts even where the impulse to exhibit this major growing up event has been strongly supported.

Preparation for menarche can dispel some of the confusion and create the readiness for comfortable understanding. To "know" about menstruation requires emotional understanding as well as a comprehension of the facts—knowledge which develops by mastering the experience itself. The facts themselves are not only complex; they are inevitably connected to questions and issues about birth, sexuality, femininity, body imagery, identity and one's social role. It is, therefore, understandable that, despite the best preparation, ideas and feelings about menarche have some elements of confusion and mystery.

Preparation will naturally include the attitudes of significant others to the body changes which precede menarche. Of particular importance here is the acceptance by the adults of becoming a woman. Significant others will include the girl's peers, who may initiate, participate with, and share in the preparation and the event. The peer group's response to the girl's body changes may include competition, support, teasing, giggling, playfulness, avoidance and celebration.

All of this occurs in the context of general sociocultural attitudes which are prominent at a given time. Societies and groups ritualize and institutionalize menarche in different ways, influencing the progress from childhood to adolescence. Our society's attitudes about femininity are undergoing significant changes, which have influenced institutional factors surrounding menarche. More sexual information is provided by schools and groups than in the past. Sexual matters are more openly portrayed. The paraphernalia for managing menstruation is advertised widely in all media. It is difficult to say what impact this new openness has upon attitudes, though changed sexual behaviors are occurring. It is important to note, however, that these changes are not universal and are reflected differently in the many subgroups in our society.

Roxanne

The following is an excerpt from the treatment of Roxanne, a 12-year-old girl. The treatment session which follows occurred about one year after referral for fighting, poor academic achievement and isolation. Over the year's time, she had improved considerably in her school work and made several friends. She had obviously developed a warm relationship with her female therapist, although it was often difficult for Roxanne to reveal feelings.

As we were walking to my office, Roxanne said, "Look at that lady's dress," referring to a woman walking ahead of us, who was wearing a sun-back dress. I replied that I wasn't sure what she was referring to.

Roxanne: All that skin.
Therapist: You don't like that?
Roxanne: No, the front is even worse. It comes down and you can see the crack.
Therapist: I'm not sure I understand.
Roxanne: That's sexy.
Therapist: Oh.
Roxanne: I'm not going to be sexy. My mother isn't sexy and she wouldn't buy me a dress like that.
Therapist: No?

Roxanne: My mother buys all my dresses for me.
Therapist: You don't choose?
Roxanne: Well, I buy my school dresses, and my mother buys the rest. She buys my swimming suits, too.
Therapist: What kind?
Roxanne: They're always high in the front, you know, and in the back, too.
Therapist: I wonder if you think it's bad to show. . . .
Roxanne: It's something you should only show in private.
Therapist: In private?
Roxanne: Well . . . it's not good to show it to any man or boy. . . . my mother says, if I ever go out with a boy and start to have a baby, she'll never have anything to do with me again. I'd have to leave the house, and she'd never talk to me again, she said.

When I wondered why this had come up, she became rather shy and said, "It's not the kind of thing to talk about." Nevertheless, she then informed me that six days earlier, she had menstruated for the first time; it had started and stopped the same day. I acknowledged her embarrassment and commented that she was growing up. Clearly uncomfortable, she turned to our typical "hangman" game. While counting the dashes for the word, she asked me how to spell "chocolate." Her reference to chocolate related to earlier occasions when I'd bought chocolate for us—on her birthday and at Christmas time. When she began to ask for chocolate at each session, I had explained that it was only for special occasions. I asked if she would like to celebrate her first menstruation with some hot chocolate. She nodded eagerly.

While we were drinking the chocolate, I asked Roxanne what she knew about menstruation, and she proceeded to tell me. Having seen the Girl Scout film on menstruation, she knew most of the facts accurately; however, she did not understand a number of things, including the reason for the loss of blood. We talked briefly about that. Becoming uncomfortable again, she said she wasn't going to get married until she was 25 years old. I wondered why.

Roxanne: Because my mother said I shouldn't get married until then.

Therapist: What do you think:

Roxanne: Well, I'm not gonna wear low dresses like that lady.

Therapist: How come?

Roxanne: Well, my mother wouldn't want me to wear dresses like that. . . . And, I don't even know if I want to get married, because I don't want to be sexy.

Therapist: (waited)

Roxanne: I do want to have children, though, and be a mother. But, I probably won't do that either. . . . Anyway, I don't really want to grow up.

Again, she looked unhappy briefly, but then told me that she would like to have three children—two boys and a girl. She hoped to have the two boys first, because she thought that the youngest in the family got spoiled. "You know who's spoiled in our family, don't you?" she asked, implying her two younger brothers. The conversation stopped, and I commented that her first menstruation was a big event, with many different feelings which we could talk about.

During the remainder of the hour, Roxanne seemed quite happy and continued to play the hangman game. She chose words which were the birthdays of famous people and July Fourth, commenting that it was the birthday of the United States.

Discussion

We are not concerned here with the ways in which the therapist works with Roxanne; our interest is primarily developmental. In this one hour, Roxanne reveals many common elements surrounding the first menstrual period. While the themes are quite typical, Roxanne's portrayal is obviously influenced by her unique experiences and problems.

In reviewing the hour, it becomes clear that Roxanne announces immediately that the major topic of the day is sex and menstruation. While the woman with the bare-back dress fortuitously provides Roxanne with the opportunity to introduce her subject, she would have undoubtedly found some way to present her concerns were this stimulus absent.

For safety's sake, Roxanne opens with a disclaimer: Isn't it awful that the lady is showing "all that skin"? The disclaimer serves many functions: It permits her to express her ambivalence, to agree with her mother that sex is unacceptable and to check what her therapist's views might be.

Throughout the hour, we can observe Roxanne moving backward and forward, from the old and familiar to the new and the changing. As soon as she has disapproved of too much exposure, she can reveal her own secret. This is immediately followed by her choice of a familiar game which also involves guessing a secret word. Having yielded her secret, she wants to be "fed" in a style connected with celebrations and special events. The regression-progression continuum is maintained in returning to an old familiar style, while the celebration itself contains the message of birth and birthdays. It is while they are drinking the chocolate that Roxanne and her therapist can discuss the subject further.

Cognitive clarity and confusion sit side by side. Menstruation, marriage and motherhood are, in fact, linked for Roxanne, but the intervening steps between each remain vague. There are rapid shifts from menstruation to marriage, to sexiness, to motherhood, to growing up—each of which is presented ambivalently. At the hour's end, the quiet, the game, the repetitive association to birthday celebrations suggest that Roxanne has begun working towards further growth.

SUMMARY

We have discussed and illustrated a variety of developmental stresses which occur in the lives of almost all children. Such events punctuate normal progression, leaving an impact on the child's evolving character. Stress mobilizes the child's coping capacities, leaving residuals of mastery and confidence. However, where the stress has not been smoothly integrated, it can create vulnerabilities and filters for future experiences.

While we have included such normative stresses as the loss of a tooth, a first camp experience, the birth of a sibling, menarche, and hospitalization, these are not the only stresses children typically experience in growing up. Entry into school, parental vacations, illness of parents or siblings, and moves are among the other typical events whose effects are important and must be understood as part of the developmental history of any child.

FURTHER READING

Bowlby, John, Robertson, James and Rosenbluth, Dina (1952), A Two Year Old Goes to the Hospital. *Psychoanalytic Study of the Child,* 7:82-94.

Fraiberg, Selma (1950), On the Sleep Disturbances of Early Childhood. *Psychoanalytic Study of the Child,* 5:285-309.

Fraiberg, Selma (1951), Enlightenment and Confusion. *Psychoanalytic Study of the Child,* 6:325-335.

Freud, Anna (1952), The Role of Bodily Illness in the Mental Life of Children. *Psychoanalytic Study of the Child,* 7:69-81.

Freud, Anna (1965), *Normality and Pathology in Childhood.* New York: International Universities Press.

Greenacre, Phyllis (1956), Reevaluation of the Process of Working-Through. *International Journal of Psycho-Analysis,* 37:43-444.

Lewis, Harold (1958), The Effect of Shedding the First Deciduous Tooth Upon the Passing of the Oedipus Complex in the Male. *Journal of the American Psychiatric Association,* 6:5-37.

Lipton, Samuel (1962), On the Psychology of Childhood Tonsillectomy. *Psychoanalytic Study of the Child,* 17:363-417.

Mason, Edward (1965), The Hospitalized Child—His Emotional Needs. *New England Journal of Medicine,* 272:406-414.

Nagera, Humberto (1966), Sleep and Its Disturbances Approached Developmentally. *Psychoanalytic Study of the Child,* 21:393-447.

Spitz, René (1945), On Hospitalism. *Psychoanalytic Study of the Child,* 1:53-74.

II

PRACTICE PRINCIPLES

3

Special Aspects of

Treatment of Children

In order to treat patients effectively, it is important to "see with the other person's eyes" as well as with one's own. This is the essence of the quality of empathy which many writers have discussed. In order to understand the child's world empathically, the adult therapist must be capable of temporary regressions. The therapist will need to be able to "grow smaller" if he or she is to see the world through the child's eyes. The child's view of the world and the place of treatment in it will naturally be different from that of the adult. Understanding these differences will help the therapist's initial efforts to develop a sound working relationship with the child and the family. This next section outlines some of the differences which distinguish child from adult patients.

1) *The child is not usually the applicant.* The child's understanding of what is wrong and what might help is, more often than not, significantly different from the adults who apply in his behalf. Although adult patients cannot present the unconscious conflicts which may have led to their seeking help, they can verbalize *some* request which initiates the treatment. With children, however, this may not be the case. For example, a 12-year-old boy was brought by his mother for his inability to do well in school despite good intellect. At the end of the first hour, the boy said, "My parents never give me what I want; I've been wanting a camera for months—can you

help me get it?" Further work with this boy shed light on his opening complaint and request. He experienced his parents as unwilling to listen to and provide for his needs. Later, the request for the camera could be understood as this youngster's difficulty with and wish to better retain images and information, clearly connected to his learning problem.

2) *Typically, a child comes for treatment because his behavior— often beyond his control—is troublesome to someone else in the community.* Thus, the parent, the teacher, the physician or other caretaker usually provides the first introduction to the child's difficulty. Such reports, however, may or may not accurately reflect the child's concerns. At her wits' end about her child's perpetual soiling, the mother can report her own distress, but what can she tell of the youngester's anger, shame or fear of his own body? The teacher can tell how upset and distracted she is by her vain efforts to control the "clown" or the "bully," but can she accurately measure the child's inner restlessness, his repeated resolution to hold himself in control, his sudden rise in tension which can no longer tolerate delayed or modified expression? The probation officer can tell of a boy's repeated runaways, but can he also tell of the boy's fears that he'd better "make tracks" or he will hurt someone with whom he lives? The doctor may tell of the daily vomiting that precedes a girl's attendance at school, but does he also always know of the child's fear of leaving her home lest she not find her mother there when she returns? How can these reports reveal the internal distress, the degree of fear of loss of control, the giving up—when the child himself does not understand these feelings?

3) *The child does not know what wares we can offer and probably would not buy them, even if they were known.*

4) *The child's attention to the "troubles" may not suit the 50-minute hour or the other structural devices which normally are employed to help people in difficulty*

5) *The help offered may come at the end of a long series of efforts by other "helpers."* Children are not usually brought for psychotherapeutic help until other measures have failed. Therefore, it is not unusual for a child to expect that more discipline and punishment are in the offing.

FIGURE 12

6) *Even more than for adults, the idea that "talking will help" is a difficult concept for children to grasp.* Talk—particularly for younger children—is not the child's primary medium. To express feelings, impulses and attitudes requires a language of considerable abstraction. Hence, with children, play is used to help them express their concerns. Play *is* talk for the child and it is artificial to see play as a form of behavior divorced from talk.

The following examples illustrate this:

Eleven-and-one-half-year-old Bettina has been brought for an evaluation because she is unhappy, overeats, is defiant and steals. She is one of few Black children in a parochial school and lives with her hardworking, conscientious but sometimes impulsive mother. In the first hour, Bettina verbally hints at a variety of problems, indicating clearly that she does have some ideas about why her mother is bringing her for help.

In the second hour, she begins to play with several games and then asks to draw. In contrast to her desultory manner with the games, she works intensely at this drawing (Figure 12).

Rarely will one see a more clear statement about conflict. Through the language of a drawing, cast in religious terms, this child tells us that she constantly struggles with opposing pulls. The left side, at the least, represents her impulses, her assertiveness (grasping hands), her blackness and her latency. The right side, at minimum, portrays the pull of her uncertain conscience, the submissiveness (wings to replace hands), and the movement toward puberty. Bettina's drawing is almost a telegraphic summary of many chapters to come.

In the course of a checker game with his therapist, a boy consistently refused to move his checkers out—even though he had many opportunities to do so. As a result, he invariably lost. In this way, he was "talking" about himself in the language available to him.

Four-and-one-half-year-old Mary was brought for help because she retained bowel movements. Due to unusually heavy traffic, she arrived 20 minutes late for her regular hour. Standing sullenly in the waiting room, she made no response to her therapist's invitation to come with her. Deftly skirting the mounting will-struggle, the therapist wondered what Mary had brought with her that day. Mary brightened a bit and showed the worker the pretty rock she had and moved toward the interview room. In the room, Mary announced that she had gum, while the therapist did not. She then turned to the pick-up sticks, neatly piling the similarly colored sticks together, "so they won't get lost." Throughout this activity she passed gas and her expression remained sad and slightly sullen. Then she arranged the checkers neatly, disordered them into a mess, and stuffed them pell-mell into the checker box—"so they can't get out." From the box, she ripped small bits of colored paper, which she wiped on the sides. During the entire meeting, Mary continued to pass gas.

If one is attentive to the ordering, the messing, the tearing of bits of paper, it takes no great stretch of the imagination to "hear" this material as the child's recapitulated struggle over bowel habits and toileting. Nor is it difficult to see the relationship between earlier body struggles and the more current and typical stubbornness—particularly in the face of the frustrating loss of time with her therapist.

The child's "language" is often richer than that of the adult. With an adult, there are words, gestures, body movements, stance and expressions; however, with a child, there is not only this "language" but more to "talk with." In addition to play, the child in the treatment room can do many things which the adult cannot. Touching the therapist, slamming a door, refusing to enter the interview room, rushing to the toilet, upsetting a block structure are all forms of "talking." Adults and children use metaphors, consciously and unconsciously, to describe situations and feelings. However, the child's use of metaphor is frequently much more concrete and therefore less opaque.

For example, a nine-year-old girl could not talk directly about her fears regarding her father's return from the Army on an emergency leave when her mother suffered a "nervous breakdown" and was hospitalized. The leave occurred after the father had been away for some time. With a good deal of feeling, Jane spoke of accidentally leaving her father's photo in the pocket of her jeans, which were later washed in the washing machine. The photo emerged—"all messed up." By the use of metaphor, she conveys her anxiety about this strange person, her father, her difficulty in remembering him and her uncertainty about what to expect from him.

It is necessary to understand the child's metaphor and to respond to it in the language of the metaphor. However, on other occasions, it is equally necessary to translate the metaphor back into the language of the child's reality. For example, two days before his birthday, Roy, age ten, talks at length with his therapist about plants and animals that are growing larger. He draws many pictures of buildings which he identifies as stores in which people are shopping for presents. Throughout this play and discussion, he makes no mention of his upcoming birthday or his anticipation about it. The therapist says directly that he thinks that the drawings and ideas have something to do with the birthday. This shift from the metaphor to the reality allows Roy to discuss more openly his eager and anxious expectations about who will remember his birthday, celebrate it and give presents to him.

The foregoing examples illustrate the requirement that child therapists develop "linguistic skills" in order to understand the variety of "dialects" that children employ.

7) *A child is actually more dependent on the environment than an adult.* He has far greater need for caretakers and is subject, in much larger measure, to the vicissitudes of real events. Because this is so, therapy with children often includes collaborative work with adults who are influential in his world. On the other hand, while dependency makes the child more vulnerable to trauma, his personality structure is less fixed, permitting greater possibilities for help.

8) *Children's symptoms are often a good deal closer to the source of conflict than they are in adults.* Naturally, less time has elapsed and the symptom is less embedded in the personality. Since everything is in flux, precise diagnosis may be difficult, but the dynamics of symptoms and their underlying conflicts may be somewhat more transparent.

For example, Debby, age nine, made frequent throat-clearing sounds. She was a sullen child who refused to mind at home, although in school she performed well. At age five, shortly before Debby was to enter school, her mother made a visit to her own dying mother in another city. Debby was left in the care of an aunt who countenanced no nonsense. Whenever she began to cry or express sadness about mother's being gone, Debby was told, "You're a big girl; stop crying." Her mother was very depressed after returning and had little energy for her daughter while mourning. At first, Debby developed nightmares which were soon replaced by the throat-clearing tic, Debby's choked expression of her anger and sadness.

FURTHER READING

Anthony, E. James (1964), Communicating Therapeutically with a Child. *Journal of the American Academy of Child Psychiatry*, 3:102-125.

Bornstein, Berta (1948), Emotional Barriers in the Understanding and Therapy of Children. *American Journal of Orthopsychiatry*, 18:691-697.

Caruth, Elaine and Ekstein, Rudolph (1966), Interpretations within the Metaphor. *Journal of the American Academy of Child Psychiatry*, 5:35-45.

Gardner, R. (1971), *Therapeutic Communications with Children*. New York: Science House.

Olden, Christine (1958), On Adult Empathy with Children. *Psychoanalytic Study of the Child*, 8:111-126.

4

Questions Beginners Ask

While the differences we have portrayed between children and adults are important for the beginner to keep in mind, they do not tell the reader precisely how to behave when meeting a child patient. Unfortunately, our theory cannot yet be translated into firm rules about treatment techniques or dispositional planning. Theoretical concepts provide an important frame of reference, offering broad guidelines for practice. But practice proficiency with patients requires repeated experiences with their attendant successes and failures. The gradual accumulation of practice experience, tested against theoretical concepts and the specific problems posed by each human being, is necessary for the development of therapeutic skill.

In the preceding section, we have attempted to delineate one set of ideas to guide the beginning worker in the actual contact with children in difficulty. Another set of ideas helpful to the new therapist can be found in the questions frequently asked by beginning clinical students. In our experience these include:

1) How do I determine whether or not a particular child needs treatment? What is a transient developmental problem as distinguished from difficulties which are likely to persist and intensify? Would the treatment of significant figures in the child's environment prove just as effective?

2) How does the child convey psychological distress?

3) How can one treat a resistant child?

4) Are there certain children with whom one can beneficially intervene on a short-term basis?

5) How does one determine whether to work with the parents and, if so, for what objectives and in what way?

6) Does the child need a changed environment such as a different school, or a placement away from home?

7) How often should the child be seen?

8) What is the proper mode of treatment: individual? family? group? or some combination?

These are difficult and challenging questions, more easily asked than answered. It is particularly difficult to answer them in general terms without reference to a specific case. However, these appropriately posed questions can be considered in the following ways.

1) *How do I determine whether or not a particular child needs treatment?* What is a transient developmental problem as distinguished from difficulties which are likely to persist and intensify? Would the treatment of significant figures in the child's environment prove just as effective?

Viewing a case through the prisms of general theoretical principles of development, psychodynamics and psychopathology is certainly useful but, in addition, each case must be decided on its own merits. The more fixed agency policies are in dictating who can receive help—in what order or in what manner—the less freedom there is to scrutinize each case for its special needs and its unique requirements.

To illustrate—an agency which refuses help to children who are not accompanied by a parent will fail to reach those who, although their numbers may be small, can use help alone. A similar disservice results when agencies dictate that both a child and his parent must see the same therapist or that each must see a different therapist. Such unbending policies are not in the best interests of our large and varied patient populations.

No child's case can be truly understood without appraising the child himself. Years ago (and even today, in some countries) women could not be seen in person by their physicians. Husbands recounted their wives' symptoms and carried home the physician's recommendations. Today, we consider this approach as inferior practice—and rightly so; yet in certain quarters minors are "treated" in an identical fashion.

In appraising each case, one must review the specific and unique life history of each child, including constitutional endowment, the child's current functioning and the quality of the child's environment. Decisions about whether to treat a child must rest upon a good "diagnosis." Although initially tentative and always subject to revision and change, a good diagnosis looks at the child from many points of view, evaluating what can be expected for the child's age and developmental stage. These should include cognitive abilities and achievements; range and depth of affective life; interpersonal modes and functions; and certain environmental factors which may advance or retard the treatment effort. Each of these categories is examined in light of the details of the child's day-to-day behavior and activities (eating, sleeping, learning, playing, etc.), and no evaluation of difficulties would be complete without equal attention to the developmental gains and personality strengths. It is this detailed inquiry and assessment which begins to sort out whether a child's problems are transient or whether they are likely to impede further psychological development.

For example, Tommy, age two and one-half, developed an acute sleep disturbance following a three-day hospitalization for croup. During the three days, he was abruptly and completely separated from his mother and isolated in a mist tent. When he returned home, he could not be put to bed easily and would awaken frequently during the night screaming in terror. A thorough assessment of Tommy's development to that point suggested that he was a bright and delightful child. There was no evidence of other difficulty either in the past or in other aspects of his day-to-day functioning. Yet the illness and the hospitalization had created a difficult "moment" for Tommy, temporarily impeding his normal progress. In this case, the transient disturbance could be managed by helping Tommy's parents. Brief work with the parents included a request that Tommy's mother take a short vacation from her job to help Tommy over his intensified separation anxiety. The Mother was asked to spend more time with Tommy, to sit by his bed until he could once again sleep and to "play" a variety of separation-mastery games with her son (peek-a-boo, hide-and-find-a-favorite-toy, make the Jack-in-the-box reappear, etc.). Follow-up with the mother after the acute episode revealed that the sleep disturbance cleared in a few weeks and had not recurred.

In contrast, Martha, age seven, began to show signs of reluctance about attending school. She dawdled and complained about various aches and pains. Her mother found herself increasingly irritated by the time required to persuade Martha to go off to school daily. However, she did not seek help until Martha began screaming in school one day when a classmate arrived with a casted leg. Martha's terror was so great that the teachers called her mother at work to have her come for the child. At the school's urging Martha's mother sought an evaluation. During the evaluation, Martha's mother arranged for a school transfer. Although this alleviated the panic reaction, the diagnostic evaluation revealed that the reluctance to go to school and the acute panic reaction were part of a more pervasive picture of inhibition and generalized fear which had been developing over time. Martha's difficulties were not simply a transient problem, but one requiring some sustained therapeutic intervention.

A further point on the developmental perspective in evaluating children is necessary to keep in mind. Some children show remarkable developmental leaps forward even in the face of great stress. A distinction must be made between those leaps which are adaptive and those which are accomplished at great cost to spontaneity and inner comfort. For example, Diane, age nine, is an accomplished child. She is an A student, plays a musical instrument ably, is popular at school although her friends are not close. She is precocious in almost all areas of endeavor. The clue that Diane's accomplishments are taking their toll is her persistent and intractable thumbsucking, which prompted her otherwise proud parents to seek an evaluation. A thorough assessment in this situation indicated that Diane was driven to perform outstandingly, but derived little comfort or pleasure from her achievements. In fact, her thumbsucking was one of her few sources of comfort—comfort which exacted its price in shame.

Neither a review of Diane's behavior nor the parents' insistence on their pride in her could adequately reveal whether Diane needed treatment. Close observation in the clinical setting disclosed the girl's inner distress and depression hidden under her poise and competence.

2) *How does the child convey psychological distress?* Individuals convey pain differently and in keeping with their age, innate capacities, culture and life experience. This is true for children as well as for adults. The specific manner in which each child conveys distress is always unique; however, distress signals tend to cluster in certain general groupings. These include:

  a) *Disturbances related to bodily functions*: eating, sleeping, bowel and bladder functions, speech, motor and perceptual abnormalities, etc.
  b) *Disturbances related to cognitive functions*: precocity, learning failure, disturbances in thinking, memory, awareness.
  c) *Disturbances in affective behavior*: fearful, anxious, depressive symptoms, hypochondriacal behavior, etc., uncontrollable crying, separation anxiety.
  d) *Disturbances in social behavior*: aggressive behavior, antisocial behavior, oppositional, isolating behavior.

Clearly such a checklist is insufficient by itself. The degree, pervasiveness, frequency and duration of symptoms and difficulties must be considered along with the impact of these in distorting personality growth and developmental progress.

3) *How can one treat a resistant child?* The treatment of a child who seems entirely reluctant and resistant is a particularly taxing and challenging problem. Assuming that the preparation has been done well with both child and parents and that the child's resistant statements do not merely reflect face-saving maneuvers, one bows to the constitutional right of all humans to determine when, how and from whom they choose to seek help. Unless the child's safety is in danger or others may be harmed, there is no way one can force a child or parent to enter into or continue treatment—no matter how fiercely one may wish to help. However, experience informs us that resistance

and reluctance, when well handled, are likely to decrease and yield in both children and adults, as this initial interchange with a 15½-year-old boy illustrates:

Therapist: What can I do for you?

Boy: (Sullenly) Nothing.

Therapist: Can you tell me then why you are here?

Boy: (Angrily) My parents made me come.

Therapist: Then they are worried. Can you say what they are worried about then?

Boy: (Challengingly) They think I have a problem—a problem about masturbating in girls' clothes, but *I* don't think it's a problem!

Therapist: (Matter-of-factly) In that case, how is it that you are here?

Boy: They forced me to come—you can't argue with my parents. It's just easier to come than fight with them. If they want me to come, I'll just come. It's easier.

Therapist: Well, we have 45 minutes every week. How would you like to spend the time?

Boy: Huh?

Therapist: We can talk . . . or if you prefer, there are games in the cabinet you can look over. . . .

Boy: Let's talk.

Therapist: What shall we talk about?

*Boy*s (Haltingly) The masturbation. . . ?

Resistances do not occur only at the initial stages of evaluation and treatment, nor do they merely address questions about continuing or discontinuing. In all treatments and at every stage of treatment, resistance to change, to new ideas and to new patterns of behavior must occur and comprise a significant part of the ongoing work. It is uncomfortable, but essential for beginners to recognize that successful resolution of initial resistance is hardly the end of that affair. Beginners often believe that any evidence of resistance subsequent to the establishment of a good working alliance proves the therapist's incompetence. The recognition that resistance is both necessary and ubiquitous develops slowly and often painfully. Beginners tend to be so uncomfortable with this idea that they frequently fail to see resistances, even when they are otherwise good observers. Even when they note them accurately, beginners often have difficulty in reacting and responding to resistances in an effective way.

4) *Are there certain children with whom 'one can beneficially intervene on a short-term basis?* The issue of long-term or brief treatment remains a muddled affair. Precise definitions are lacking and advocates for one or another style are endlessly involved in ideological debate. As professionals are faced with larger numbers of patients and demands upon professional time, there has been a recent and understandable trend toward brief intervention. This trend is derived from a growing body of knowledge based upon stress and life crisis theory as well as being influenced by political and logistical pressures. It is our view that neither the short- nor the long-term ideology can cover all cases and situations.

Clearly, very impaired youngsters whose disturbance is chronic and severe will usually require longer care. Conversely, children who have been subject to recent trauma and whose difficulties do not pervade multiple areas of personality may be amenable to a more focal and brief approach. The decision is often not easy and requires attention to various factors, which include:

a) How recent was the onset of symptoms and/or the stressful event? Is the disturbance related to and will it complicate an emerging developmental phase and task?

b) What is the history of the child's previous adaptation to stress? Different children recover at different rates. If available, a prior history of "recoverability" is most useful.

c) Despite the difficulties, are there evidences of symptom reduction, flexibility and shifts in defensive and coping mechanisms already in progress? Such evidence at the beginning phase of treatment may speak to the feasibility of a brief approach.

d) And, of course, the reality of the family's circumstances, motivation and willingness to assist must be taken into account.

It happens all too often that inadequate attention is paid to what the child and the parents want and what they are prepared to tolerate. The error falls on both sides: We end up providing either less than is needed or far more than is wanted or useful.

5) *How does one determine whether to work with the parents and, if so, for what objectives and in what way?* Work with parents and other significant family members is important in helping children. This aspect of the work will be discussed in Part III on Clinical Beginnings. However, a few general observations are worth noting here.

As indicated, children are more dependent than adults upon people in their lives for care, guidance and sustenance. It is not useful to view children as incomplete adults nor to pay insufficient attention to the reality of the child's developmental stage. Both factors argue for work with the parents regarding:

a) The maintenance of an alliance with the family for the continued support of the child's treatment;

b) A continuing flow of pertinent information about the child's current activities and experiences. The younger the child, the less likely is the therapist to hear from the child directly about day-to-day events and experiences;

c) The common task of parent and therapist to create or modify those aspects of the child's outer world which may either fuel the disturbance or impede the child's growth. At times, this may require helping the parent change real circumstances such as altering sleeping arrangements or changing a school. At other times the therapist must help the parent modify attitudes and behavior which interfere with the child's development. This is, of course, the most complicated aspect of work with parents.

Few children can be treated without parental assistance. At a minimum, the parent must consent and make the necessary arrangements for the child's regular appointments and for the payment of fees. As a general principle, therefore, regular meetings with parents are called for, unless there are sound and persuasive clinical reasons for doing otherwise.

Once again, there are no fixed rules which can determine the exact plan of work with different parents in different circumstances. This applies to questions of frequency, purpose and the therapist's style of work. It applies as well to decisions about whether the child's therapist should maintain regular contact with the parents or whether a collaborative worker should carry this major responsibility. Our experience, which has included both approaches, suggests that, in most instances, the collateral work with the parents is best done by the child's therapist, unless clinical determinants suggest otherwise. These include not only the developmental and psychodynamic issues of the case, but the therapist's comfort with this way of working. Least significant are rigid administrative policies.

One last comment here: All too often, contact with the child's parents becomes the game of "who is to blame?" Beginning therapists tend to view parents—often unconsciously—as the "culprits" of their child's drama. To convey this attitude to parents—especially if they are already apprehensive about such an implication—almost guarantees treatment troubles. It would be hard to emphasize too strongly the importance of tact and empathy in the contacts with parents. Depending upon how it is done, work with the parents can aid immeasurably in facilitating the child's treatment or can create insurmountable, self-generated obstacles.

6) *Does the child need a changed environment such as a different school, or a placement away from home?* We have already made the point that the environment in which the child lives is critical in helping or hindering progress. There are, unfortunately, external factors over which the child has no control and which may be so noxious that progress is impossible without major alteration. For example, when the treatment is designed to enhance the child's sense of safety, stability, curiosity and belief in his own worth and effectiveness, and the environment is unalterably full of danger, chaos, depreciation and punishment, treatment faces impossible odds.

As noted earlier, a thorough assessment requires an understanding of the child *and* the world outside. Decisions that treatment cannot work without a major environmental change should not be arrived at hastily or without good evidence. In most instances, one can be helpful to the child even when the world in which he lives is far from perfect. However, there are times when the difficult and painful conclusion that treatment alone cannot help becomes obvious. In some instances, good judgment requires that the responsible adults be told forthrightly that treatment cannot be effective at this time, in these circumstances. On rarer occasions, the child therapist must become a more active agent in the child's behalf. When the child is in such jeopardy that life and safety are threatened, it may be necessary to enlist the help of legal and other authorities to insure the child's welfare. Such direct advocacy must rest on three factors:

a) clear and present danger for or from the child;
b) the certainty that other responsible adults cannot or will not act; and
c) the certainty that a more salutary alternative actually exists.

It is an unhappy reality that not all problems have solutions. Too often conditions a) and b) may be met with c) unfulfillable. Occasionally, psychotherapy attempts the unsolvable because of reluctance to acknowledge that nothing effective can be done.

7) *How often should the child be seen?* Frequency of appointments cannot be prescribed without attention to the task, the request of the family, the circumstances and the diagnostic assessment. However, the following principles are generally applicable. Whatever the frequency, the appointments should be regular, clearly understood by all concerned, and, if possible, at the same time and in the same place. Most of the time, therapeutic work cannot proceed at a reasonable pace at less than weekly intervals. While there is nothing sacred about the once-weekly contact or the 50-minute hour, such scheduling has become commonplace out of decades of experience with anguished people. Many psychological problems are rooted in disorder, inconsistency and unreliability, and the difficulty human beings experience in establishing close and important connections with others. It is these disorders that psychotherapy tries to deal with. The patterning of meetings at least weekly for appropriate durations of time is one of our important tools. In addition, psychotherapeutic work depends upon the sense of continuity from session to session which is hampered by long intervals. Consequently, most considerations of

frequency revolve around whether this particular child and his family can profit from weekly or more frequent sessions.

8) *What is the proper mode of treatment: individual? family? group? or some combination?* Clearly, different people profit from different therapeutic experiences. This is as true for children and adolescents as it is for adults. There was a time when sharp distinctions were made between intrapsychic and interpersonal disorders leading to equally sharp distinctions among modes of treatment presumably aimed more fully at one or the other. Over time, and with considerable inquiry and experience, these distinctions have become less clear. While the debate persists over the superiority of one or another treatment mode, we are convinced that no one system has captured a corner on therapeutic wisdom.

However, our experience in training beginning therapists suggests that they can learn their craft best by treating individuals first. In the same way that many patients profit from the privacy and undivided attention inherent in individual sessions, the novice therapist gains knowledge and skill from the opportunity to observe and interact closely with one person at a time. We think that the techniques needed for more complex tasks of working with families and groups are built upon the foundation gained in individual treatment. However, even when individual treatment is chosen as the primary mode, valuable information may be gathered from the opportunity to observe the child in group situations. Some treatment agencies have productively used home visits, family sessions and peer-group situations as part of the diagnostic assessment.

Although we have indicated that the concepts of the intrapsychic vs. interpersonal disturbances cannot be sharply demarcated, these are useful, in a gross way, in the determination of which mode or combination of modes can be most effectively used.

Generally, individual treatment permits greater opportunity for unravelling perplexing, internal conflicts and disturbing fantasies. Worrisome and shameful private concerns are more likely to be revealed when the child begins to experience the therapist as a safe and nonjudgmental confidant. The unconscious bases for symptoms or maladaptive behavior are more likely to surface and become available for exploration and resolution as part of the powerful emotional experience of the one-to-one session.

Family and group situations have their own power but tend to permit greater opportunities to focus upon problems of interrelationships, communication and socialization.

In all treatment situations, how problems are conceptualized is a matter of emphasis rather than a statement of absolute verity. What cannot be conveyed in any discussion about the choice of treatment modes is the differing quality of the affective experience. Beginners tend to believe that a cognitive understanding of the problems translated into appropriate verbal interventions in an appropriate mode of treatment will remedy the child's difficulty. Whatever the mode, treatment is not a discussion; it is, instead, the experience of trying out new patterns in the context of a safe but powerful emotional relationship, be it with an individual therapist, the family group or the peer group.

FURTHER READING

Anthony, E. James (1974), Child Therapy Techniques. In: *American Handbook of Psychiatry*, New York: Basic Books.
Brody, Sylvia (1964), Aims and Methods in Child Psychotherapy. *Journal of the American Academy of Child Psychiatry*, 3:385-412.

5

Practice and Protocol

Although "cookbook" injunctions and recommendations have their limitations, experience suggests that some simple "dos and don'ts" can forewarn the novice of common errors in beginning work.

SUPERVISION

Every beginning therapist experiences some anxiety initially. A great deal of conceptual and experiential knowledge, as well as practical skills, is essential for effective work. Such knowledge and skill can be accrued only gradually, over a period of time . . . but one must begin *now*. Lacking wide clinical experience and the integration of theory and practice, a helpful "tutor" is essential. For this reason, the importance of the supervisor—the experienced worker—cannot be overemphasized.

Even before beginning the first cases, it is useful to take questions and concerns to the supervisor, who can guide and initiate gently, offering sufficient supports and direction without restricting the beginner's natural intuition, curiosity and endowments. Good supervision is the process through which theory becomes applicable and practical. Psychotherapeutic work cannot be learned from books and "courses" alone. It is learned in the doing and in the give-and-take between beginner and experienced clinician. Supervisory sessions are probably the best setting in which the specifics of a "case" can be translated into general, theoretical principles and then translated back to the specific psychotherapeutic task.

The natural anxiety of the beginning student is to imagine that the supervisor expects high levels of competence and theoretical proficiency. This anxiety is frequently experienced either as a reluctance to expose doubts and uncertainty or to over-theorize and to endow the supervisor with magical, theoretical wisdom. By and large, most supervisors recognize that beginners are beginners and that theory serves only as a general guidepost which can illuminate but which can also obstruct understanding when used rigidly. Supervisors are familiar with the beginner's tendency to see only what one expects to see theoretically and the potential to overlook what is actually there to be seen.

"HOMEWORK"

In approaching a case, it is valuable to review all the material on hand. Sometimes, beginners fear that such a review will contaminate their impressions of the people they are about to meet. This attitude tends to grow in direct proportion to the bulk of preexisting material. Beginners, fearful that they will not be able to capture spontaneous and firsthand impressions, avoid prior data, particularly if they are in the form of another therapist's diagnostic impressions. Although understandable, this fear that someone else's perceptions will become a personal straitjacket leaves the beginner with less information about how to proceed. By and large, ignorance is not bliss. In our experience, most beginning therapists have been able to trust their own impressions and sort these from others' judgments.

Therefore, we recommend that certain types of preparatory work can be most productive. In addition to simply reading and digesting the material, we have found that all therapists profit from beginning the process of observing the data from various perspectives, and developing initial inferences and hypothesis which will, however, require testing out with the patient. Contrary to the idea that review will constrain understanding, a playful approach to case review can expand vision. "By "playful," we do not mean a lack of rigor or discipline; we refer instead to that quality of the mind which can consider various alternatives, holding each in speculative suspension until the patient confirms or refutes hypotheses.

An aid in this process is a "reorganization" of the data in particular ways. One reorganization schema which our students have found useful is what we have come to call the "existential flow sheet." This involves clustering historical information in the following way:

Date	Age	Event	Context

Even where historical and developmental data are obtained in the most orderly way, this information emerges in fragments at different moments in an interview or over a series of interviews. For example, one may hear the story of a child's first attendance at school at one time and the story of a grandparent's death much later in a parent's account. It is all too easy to miss the link between such events. The "existential flow sheet" helps the therapist make appropriate links and, for instance, discover that the two experiences mentioned by the parent have occurred in the same month. Also, we frequently get longitudinal accounts without sufficient cross-sectional views. The cross-sectional view permits a different and sometimes more useful sense of the gestalt of experience.

As an example, the following are segments from such a flow sheet:

Date	Age	Event	Context
Oct. 19, 1959	0	Birth	Parents unmarried. First child of 22-year-old mother. Couple in conflict.
Oct. - Jan. 1960	0 - 4 mos.	Colic	Parental relationship dissolved. Father leaves area when child is 2 months old.
Sept. 1962	2 yrs. 11 mos.	Starts at day care center	Mother begins full-time work. Caretaking of child prior to day care center unclear.
Feb. 1965	5 yrs. 4 mos.	Enuresis occurs	Mother married several months prior.
Dec. 1967	8 yrs. 2 mos.	Juvenile diabetes is discovered on routine physical	Mother promoted to administrative job. Stepfather resumes education via night school. Grandmother visits for Christmas.

July - Sept. 1968	8 yrs. 9 mos.	Summer away at "diabetic" camp	Mother's job begins to involve travel.
Jan. 1973	13 yrs. 3 mos.	Menarche	Family moves and girl begins at new school. Mother and step-father quarreling. Girl discovers her illegitimacy. Parents divorce shortly thereafter.
Sept. 1975	15 yrs. 11 mos.	Girl becomes pregnant and miscarries	Past few years marked by mother's having several affairs. Diabetes less in control, with increased need for insulin.
Feb. 1976	16 yrs. 5 mos.	Seeks treatment when discovers she is pregnant again	Mother and daughter growing further apart.

This historical material was part of a great deal of information obtained during one interview with the girl and later interview with the mother. It is apparent from the above reorganization of the data that many important events and experiences were contiguous in time though they were not presented together during these first two in-terviews. Some of the material was given by the mother and some came from the patient. The flow sheet permits links to be discovered between experiences, raising speculative questions and areas for fur-ther inquiry. For example, the history of the patient's diabetes was presented by the mother as a detailed and well-organized, medical story. The girl's awareness of her mother's affairs was offered by the girl with considerable distress. The relationship between this emo-tional stress and the instability of the diabetic condition was not presented by mother or daughter as a potentially linked situation. These possible connections become evident as the material is viewed with some order and system.

Looking at the data in an effort to discern developmental gestalts, as above, promotes hypothesizing about the possible relationships be-tween loss, illness, menarche, a sense of unreliable body integrity and the mother's affairs. All these may be important in the girl's doubts about her body and its sexuality and the attendant pregnancies.

We do not mean to imply that historical information is the only material which lends itself to the process of orderly inference making or that a complete history must be obtained before beginning to think about the patient. While it is unquestionable that inferences stand on firmer ground when buttressed by information, it must be acknowledge that a "complete" or an "undistorted" history is an ideal—never quite achievable.

Even the smallest amount of information can provide the stimulus for speculation and beginning hypotheses. Such first speculations should not be viewed as merely an entertaiinng intellectual activity. Rather, they serve as a way of preparing to receive and evaluate further information and, particularly for the beginner, as a continuing exercise in developing fluent, clinical thinking. However, the value of such early playful speculation must always be tempered by an awareness of the dangers of "parlor analysis." One can become so enchanted with one's brilliance that what is never more than a hunch becomes a certainty.

The first information which is generally available is typically provided in a telephone inquiry about possible service. Some agencies utilize a form for recording this telephone contact; some may follow up with an application form or a "screening" interview. Whatever the initial procedure, the information from these sources is valuable and should be reviewed carefully as "homework" for the next steps.

For example, the following illustrations consist of material gathered at the time of the initial phone call or drop-in visit requesting service and the application for treatment filled out by the parent shortly after the initial contact.

Suzanne

From the information provided by the phone contact, we can begin to consider the following:

This appears to be an intact family, whose address tells us that they reside in a middle-class neighborhood. We also know that Suzanne is in an appropriate grade for her age and that the school she attends is an ethnically diverse one.

On another level, we know that Suzanne's difficulties are at least of three years' duration and that the mother can observe that Suzanne's problems are not exclusively related to school attendance.

Date_____ 11-14-75 _____

Taken by_____ Intake Worker _____

Referred by__ Mother's Friend _____

INTAKE FOR CHILDREN'S SERVICE

CHILD'S NAME_____ Suzanne _____ Age__9___ M____ F_X__

Family Address_____ 1930 43rd Street _____ Telephone_____ 569-2176 _____

School_____ Cleveland Elementary _____ Grade_H3_____ Teacher_____

Birthdate_____ 1-10-66 _____ Birthplace___ San Francisco _____

FAMILY:	Name	Age	Occupation or School
Father_____	George		Salesman
Mother_____	Anna		Housewife

Marital status of parents_____

Stepparent_____

Siblings_____ Brother, 11 3/4 _____

Family doctor_____ Dr. Brown (Pediatrician) _____

Previous psychiatric contact____ None _____

Request and disposition:

Mother called: Trouble started in first grade, stomachaches, vomiting in order to avoid going to school. "Has trouble going away from me." Always worried. Insists mother pick child up.	Application sent (date)_____ 11-15-75 _____ Application returned_____ 11-20-75 _____ Information requested (date and from whom)_____

Dr. Brown talking to child approximately weekly. It has helped some -- but problem still there and mother wanted a psychiatrist to look.

Application for Psychiatric Treatment

Date _19 November 1975_

CHILD'S NAME _Suzanne_   Birthdate _1 Oct 66_   Birthplace _S. F._

Home Address _1930 43rd St._   Home Phone _569-2176_

School _Cleveland_   School Grade _H-3rd_   Religion _Jewish_

FAMILY

	Name	Birthdate	Birthplace	School or Occupation
Mother	_Anna_	_6 May '34_	_Germany_	_Housewife_
Father	_Georg_	_21 Apr '31_	_Germany_	
Sisters and/or Brothers	_Michael_	_14 Feb '63_	_S. F._	_Jr High_

Others living in family (include relationship to child)_____

Who referred you to the clinic? _A friend_

How long have you lived in San Francisco?_____

CHIEF PROBLEM _Unnatural dependence on mother_ _stomach aches_

When did it first occur? _February 1972_

MEDICAL

(A recent physical examination is a necessary step for admission to the clinic)

Name of Physician _Dr. Brown_   Address _5 Church St._

Date of child's most recent general physical exam _February 1975_

Is child receiving medical treatment now, and if so, for what? _Yes - for_ _her stomach aches_

If father does not live at home, list present address and phone number:

_____

The family has sought help from their pediatrician, who apparently recognized the psychological nature of this child's "organic" problems—though he attempted to manage these himself. There is a hint that the mother is no longer satisfied with this arrangement and wants more expert help. We do not know why she has chosen this moment to ask for additional help.

We also note that Suzanne is the only girl and the younger of two children. We can wonder whether this position in the family contributes to what appears to be generalized separation problems. Finally, we note that the application form was returned promptly, providing a rough index to the family's motivation.

The application form itself provides us with further information and clues to further hypotheses. We now know the parents are Jewish immigrants, born in Nazi Germany. We do not know when they emigrated and what the impact of that experience was. However, since we already suspect that Suzanne's problems are related to separation concerns, and we know from research that survivors of the Nazi era often have had major turmoil about loss and separation, we wonder about the possible link and note this as one crucial area for inquiry and assessment.

Following the assumption that the mother has filled out the application form and that it represents a sample of her thinking and writing, we observe the following: The mother has given her husband's occupation (salesman) when talking with the intake worker, but has left that space blank on the form. We will consider whether this might be an oversight or whether there is some issue about father's work. Both children were born in San Francisco, and the family has been in the city for many years, suggesting some validation for our hunch that this is a stable family.

Mother's written statement of the chief problem is slightly different from her report on the phone. The stomachaches have now taken second place to mother's wider concern about her daughter's "unnatural dependence," though it is likely that her precise date of onset (February, 1972) refers to the stomach problems.

We are now prepared to meet the parents and the child with the understanding that critical areas for assessment will revolve around issues of dependency and autonomy, as well as closeness and separation. We will want tó explore carefully the child's development along the spectrum of separation-individuation and the possible expression of conflict through somatic symptoms. This may be a highly charged area, given the parents' origins and experiences in Germany, and will therefore require some care and tact in its assessment. We will want to ascertain to what degree this configuration of problems has influenced other areas of development, such as learning, peer relationships, and interests.

If our hunch about the mother's dissatisfaction with the pediatrician's efforts is correct, we will be alert as to whether this colors her view of other helpers, including ourselves.

Peter

The intake worker's notes inform us that Peter's mother has chosen to apply, in person, for her son. This may be especially noteworthy since her work makes it likely that she is familiar with scheduled appointments, typical of social agency procedures. Thus we may ask whether her "drop-in" is a reflection of an assertive, direct style, a clue that a decision once made must be implemented immediately, an indication of a sense of urgency and/or anxiety, her attempt to "case the joint," or some combination of these factors.

From the identifying information, we know that the mother and her three sons live in a middle-class neighborhood and that the father lives elsewhere, though we do not know when the separation occurred, where he lives and whether he maintains contact with his family. A babysitter lives in, which leads to various questions about the timing and significance of this person's presence in the household.

We note that the mother applies a few days before Peter's birthday—an impending birthday or special anniversary may often focus attention upon a child. Peter is the oldest child, and we will want to consider whether this ordinal position has been a stress in his development.

Peter is in an appropriate grade, although he has problems at school as well as at home. Problems of control seem pervasive; the mother and the school experience difficulty with Peter, and Peter himself has difficulty in managing his body. In a highly tentative way,

Date_____ 2-14-75 _____

Taken by_____ Intake Worker _____

Referred by_____ Mother via Pediatrician __

INTAKE FOR CHILDREN'S SERVICE

CHILD'S NAME____ Peter _____ Age__ 8 ___ M X __ F____
                                              Home: 376-1290
Family Address____ 496 Hamm Avenue _____ Telephone Work: 193-1040, Ext. 419

School_____ John Jay Elementary _____ Grade__H-2 ___ Teacher_____

Birthdate_____ 2-19-67 _____ Birthplace__ Sonoma _____

FAMILY:	Name	Age	Occupation or School
Father	Jerome	29	Lithographer
Mother	Jane	30	Policewoman

Marital status of parents_____ Separated _____

Stepparent_____

Siblings____ Two brothers, ages 5 and 3; has live-in baby-sitter. _____

Family doctor____ Dr. Green (Pediatrician) _____

Previous psychiatric contact____ None _____

Request and disposition:

	Application sent (date)__ 2-14-75 _____

Application returned____ 2-14-75 _____

Information requested
(date and from whom)_____

   Mother dropped in; a big woman in stature and build. Pleasantly overbearing, controlling. At first, unclear as to whether she was here to make a referral -- very composed and at ease on the surface. Son having behavior problems in shcool and at home. Theme was on "controlling him." Has eye twitch and a bed wetter. Doctor suggested she come here as result of having his eyes tested. Only at end of brief meeting says she and husband are separated; came up around subject of income.

$914 gross/month - $100 from husband a month.

Application for Psychiatric Treatment

Date___2/14/75___

CHILD'S NAME___PETER___ Birthdate_2/19/67_ Birthplace_SONOMA_

Home Address___496 HAMM AVE.___ Home Phone_376-1290_

School_JOHN JAY ELEMENTARY_ School Grade_H-2_ Religion_____

FAMILY

	Name	Birthdate	Birthplace	School or Occupation
Mother	JANE	4/3/44	S.F.	POLICEWOMAN
Father	JEROME	4/10/45	FRESNO	LITHOGRAPHER
Sisters	MARK	3/20/70	S.F.	JOHN JAY (KIND.)
and/or Brothers	PATRICK	3/23/70	S.F.	

Others living in_____DEBRA ANDREWS, baby sitter_____
family (include
relationship to child)_____

Who referred you to the clinic?___DR. JOHN GREEN_____

How long have you lived in San Francisco?___MAJOR PORTION OF LIFE___

CHIEF PROBLEM___BEHAVIOR ─── BED WETTING !!___

When did it first occur?___ALWAYS !_____

MEDICAL
(A recent physical examination is a necessary step for admission to the clinic)

Name of Physician___DR. GREEN___ Address___3 MAIN ST.___

Date of child's most recent general physical exam___OCT. 1974___

Is child receiving medical treatment now, and if so, for what?___NO___

If father does not live at home, list present address and phone number:
_____359 BERKELEY AVE., S.F. ─── NO PHONE_____

we can consider what might be the relationship between the mother's occupation and Peter's difficulty with controls. It is also worth wondering about the belated information regarding the parental separation. Information which surfaces as seemingly parenthetic often reveals an area of continuing conflict.

The application form completed subsequent to the brief screening meeting adds the following information and ideas. We learn that Peter was born elsewhere, raising questions about the circumstances and timing of the family's move. Father is in the city, though we do not yet know about his ongoing relationship to his family. The written form presents Peter's problems somewhat differently from the verbal account. The "problem" has been reduced to two words: "behavior—bedwetting." Though put more parsimoniously than the verbal report, the written presentation has a more striking effect, particularly when given as occurring "always." Questions arise about mother's sense of despair or her disgust about behavior which never seems to end. It is noteworthy that Peter's mother applies after his eye examination, though he has been bedwetting all his life.

We know that enuretic children who have never achieved bladder control are usually in greater difficulty than those who have at some time in their lives mastered this developmental task.

With all of this in mind, we may decide to focus our attention on the parental separation and its impact. In our developmental history, particular attention will be paid to the details of Peter's enuresis and disturbing behavior. Since our initial hunch suggests a rather serious set of problems, we will carefully assess his developmental achievements and abilities. These will be crucial for our diagnostic and prognostic thinking and the development of a treatment plan.

APPOINTMENTS

Some therapists prefer to arrange their appointments by phone while others prefer to use the mails. Neither method is intrinsically superior. What is important is to keep these first communications friendly, brief and clear. These should convey a welcoming readiness to meet the patient and his family. However, transactions over the phone in any extensive way should be avoided since they may hamper full utilization of the admission information for the most effective initiation of the therapeutic relationship. Appointment times are usually arranged according to mutual convenience. However, unusual requests (Saturday afternoons, pre-dawn hours and other less dramatic examples) may indicate important dynamic issues—including significant resistances—which will need to be addressed early if a treatment relationship is to begin properly.

Conveying simple information straightforwardly can alleviate patient anxiety and strain. Since we assume that most beginning therapists work in large, complicated organizations, it is useful to determine whether the patient knows where you are located and what systems have been developed to announce the patient's presence. The receptionist's greeting, the physical space in which the patient waits, and the promptness in meeting appointment times all are parts of the overall gestalt which the patient forms about the services he is to receive.

The manner of arranging initial contacts with the parents requires equally careful consideration and flexibility. Some therapists prefer to meet initially with the parents together, while others prefer to begin meeting with each, separately. Available information may suggest a preferred approach. Each approach has its own virtues and limitations. The conjoint interview will tend to reveal more about parental interaction, while the individual interviews allow more focus on each person's private concerns. A family interview may add further information about how the unit operates together. Whatever the initial approach, it should be subject to change as a broader picture emerges.

In setting appointments for either the child or the parents, directness is useful. Wherever possible, appointments should be arranged with the person involved and not through intermediaries. Naturally, some exceptions to this "principle" exist—particularly in the case of very young children or absent parents. The setting of appointments with adolescents can be particularly tricky. Unless otherwise indicated, it is probably wisest to make the appointments with the adolescent directly. Although adolescents may resist involving their parents, careful consideration of the timing, appropriateness and reasons for including or excluding parents of adolescents is essential. As indicated, some contact, at least in the initial phases of assessment, is usually necessary. There are, of course, evolving cultural and societal attitudes which influence our procedures. The recent Supreme Court decision (*Planned Parenthood of Central Missouri* v. *Danforth*, 96 S. Ct. 2861, 1976) permitting adolescents, under some conditions, to determine for themselves whether they will seek an abortion is a case in point.

Often, resistances are conveyed by absences, cancellations, and requests for appointment changes. It is impressive how frequently beginning therapists fail to observe numerous changes and missed appointments and continue to work with patients in absentia. Once this is noted, the beginner may feel awkward about discussing such meaningful events and persist in "patient pursuit" long after such outreach has become futile.

INTRODUCTIONS

The beginning moments and hours of therapy provide opportunities and pitfalls for the novice therapist. First impressions usually make a sharp impact on both the patient and the therapist. The patient who experiences the therapist as friendly but not effusive, interested but not intrusive, and thoughtful but not judgmental, will probably be off to a trusting start. Nevertheless, everyone has a characteristic "set" about meeting new people, which is often heightened in this anxiety-laden situation. For example, people who tend to be suspicious of others may cast the therapist in an unfriendly light, regardless of the therapist's actual behavior.

The natural anxiety of the therapist may obscure important observational material in these first moments of contact. Despite early unease, the therapist soon begins to notice where and how the patient sits, how the patient responds to the initial greeting, whether conversation begins immediately or not, and other postural and behavioral events, "on the way to the forum." In short, the therapeutic encounter begins when the patient arrives, not just at the point of entry into the office.

A common and particularly problematic outcome of the beginning therapist's anxiety is a tendency to adopt a pseudo-professional and impersonal stance. Such comments as: "I have been assigned your

case," or "Clinic policy dictates that . . ." are instances of such coun-
tertherapeutic approaches. It is important to remember that you are
the therapist and that you are the one who is assuming immediate
responsibility for the patient. Beginning therapists are often prone
to minimize their importance to the patient. While understandable,
such personal uncertainty should not interfere with the patient's early
relationship with the therapist as a person—not an institution—to
whom he looks for assistance.

A typical concern of beginning therapists relates to how they introduce themselves and how they address the patient. Proponents of
first name, both names, last name and title only argue vigorously for
their point of view. We have observed that anxiety often fuels polar-
ization either towards instant intimacy or stilted reliance on formality.
Any approach has its impact. We believe that ideology is not the
best determinant. The setting, the therapist's style and comfort, and,
most importantly, the available understanding and information are
better guides to introductions as well as to the treatment.

CONFIDENTIALITY

Confidentiality is a most complex issue. It is best to err—if one must
—in the direction of more, rather than less, care in this regard.
Patients are alarmed by the unintentional "loose" talk which can
occur around a switchboard or in the hallways. "Wandering" case
folders are another recurrent nightmare. The patient deserves privacy
and thoughtfulness as minimal conditions for proper treatment.

While underscoring the need for confidentiality, we must add that
parents are sometimes quite distressed over a rigid adherence to the
commandment of confidentiality taking the form of "I can't discuss
that with you. . . ." This is apt to sound like a brush-off or reprimand.
However, the question of what is confidential in the treatment of the
child, when parents are also meeting with the therapist, deserves careful consideration. This is not a simple matter since there are multiple
demands placed upon the therapist. The child's wish for utter privacy
may conflict with the parents' wish-and right to know.

In general, the "raw data" of the child's hours—his exact comments
and the play in which he engages—belong to the private interchange
between the child and the therapist. It is this principle, for instance,

which governs the agreement to hang a child's drawing on the office wall only during the actual meeting with the child. However inconvenient it is for the therapist, the pictures are typically taken down and kept safely at all other times. Simply because a child's fantasy has been presented in a tangible form does not permit its display for others' view.

However, the therapist's impressions about the child should not necessarily be kept confidential from the parent but can be conveyed with discretion, tact, and in keeping with one's assessment of how the parent will use such information. In general, parents not only have the right to know about the child's difficulties and progress, but they can become allies in helping the child consolidate the gains made in treatment. Parents need particular help in understanding and sometimes in tolerating the shifts in behavior which are a natural and frequently desirable consequence of the therapeutic work.

An equally complex issue related to confidentiality concerns what information may be transmitted back to the child from parent meetings. If these meetings are in behalf of the child and not in the service of direct treatment of the parent, a child will need to know that such meetings take place, and all the parties concerned need to understand that the therapist has the discretion to use pertinent information from the parents in order to help the child. Parents can be advised to inform their children of some of the issues they will bring to the therapist and children in treatment should be encouraged to express their curiosity, ideas and concerns about parent meetings. This very complicated aspect of child therapy will be discussed more fully in the section on work with parents.

Particular care should be taken in handling the requests of agencies, schools and other institutions for information, findings and speculations concerning a child. While such requests are usually an adjunct to the agencies' involvement with the child, it is wise to be cautious in off-the-cuff discussions—especially on the telephone—concerning any patient. Parental permission should always be obtained before holding any conversation whatsoever regarding a child—even if such conversations are with individuals known to be involved with the patient. This matter takes on increasing importance in our age of computerized data banks.

FEES

Fee setting and payment arrangements are issues which sometimes tend to be obscured by the seemingly more interesting and challenging dynamics of a case. In its simplest, least complicated form, the treatment situation involves payment for services rendered. Fees should be reviewed periodically, since they are an integral part of any treatment relationship. The fee policy should be clearly stated at the outset of treatment. In institutions which can permit a sliding fee scale, it should be related to the family's income. Wherever the treatment occurs, the fee should be realistic and reviewable.

Yet, the issue of fees and their payment involves something other than simple financial transactions. For example, a mother and child were both in treatment, each seen once a week. While the fee for the mother's appointments was paid regularly, the fee for the child's treatment was paid erratically. Obviously, something was being communicated, nonverbally, about the mother's attitudes toward herself, the child, his treatment and the therapist; to ignore this erratic payment would have been an error. In practice, one will begin to discover how patient's reactions to fees and their payment can provide a barometer of the psychological forces and the tranferences at work. Fantasies will be evoked around fee payments, and many potential situations for mutual avoidance or acting-out can arise. If the fee is reasonable and the financial circumstances of the family have not substantially changed, delinquencies or prolonged hassles regarding payment are usually clear indications of resistance. The therapist's feelings about lowering or raising fees can also be instructive signals of potential countertransference dilemmas.

SUMMARY

The work of therapy involves an interaction between two people —not between a person and an institution. It is important to communicate directly with the patient(s) and to maintain a viable working relationship with the parents. Although the individual hours with a child are strictly confidential, it is important to remember that the world in which the child lives contains highly significant others and that it is generally unwise to erect an artificial barrier between the child and his experiences in that environment. Parents, moreover, are often helpful in filling out those areas about which we know very little, both past and present, and in clarifying behavior which would otherwise escape our understanding. Finally, fees and their payment offer a vehicle through which important communications are transmitted and received, largely in nonverbal fashion. As valuable psychodynamic "comments," they are not to be underestimated in the overall picture of a case.

FURTHER READING

Sylvester, Emmy and Cooper, Shirley (1966), Truisms and Slogans in the Practice and Teaching of Child Psychotherapy. *Journal of the American Academy of Child Psychiatry*, 5:617-629.

6

Toys and Play

Toys permit a child to express concerns, interests, ideas, skills and a view of the world. Play and the "pretend" in it are the vehicles which allow this expression in a sufficiently "distant" and indirect way. This helps to promote expression without overwhelming or frightening the patient. Since play involves the imagination, it is a route toward understanding the child's fantasies, which help us comprehend the issues of importance to him.

Consequently, toys which tend to frighten or frustrate the child's expression have no place in the playroom. Toys which come apart easily require endless patience in their assembly and reassembly, beyond the skill and capacities of most children. Once complete, they become far too precious to permit easy play, exploration and use. Gadgety, easily breakable toys are also frustrating. Moreover, they often require the child to behave as a spectator rather than as an involved participant.

While the playroom need not be in impeccable drawing-room order, neither should it be in such disarray that the child or his therapist cannot readily locate wanted boys. The sloppy, cluttered playroom fails to promote that minimum order which should be established as a background in helping the child.

No two child therapists will use toys in exactly the same way—any more than two children will play exactly alike. However, it may prove helpful to adopt the following ground rules of your "play philosophy":

1) Although you may share toys with other therapists, remember to refer to them as yours.
2) Since they are yours—and *not* the depersonalized possessions of "the Hospital" or "the Clinic"—get to know the values and limits of each toy in your play space.
3) After you get new play equipment, unwrap it, discard its wrapper and assess its potential. If a child knows that he is the first to use a toy, he may overvalue that toy and disdain others.
4) Try not to create a museum but a comfortable therapeutic atmosphere in which working with toys constitutes the medium through which important issues in the child's life can be discussed and considered.
5) If you are not a museum curator, neither are you the keeper of the crown jewels. Toys do get broken and dirty. While no specific advice is appropriate in regard to "toy security" (other than replacing toys too damaged to be effective), some middle ground seems the wisest: You are not a security agent, guarding your toys against intruders; nor are you the proponent of a laissez-faire attitude toward the important materials at hand. When toys break, efforts to repair them on the spot can be useful in helping the child experience that some things are reparable.

Think about the properties of the toys in order to maximize your understanding of the child's communications. Items such as the magnifying glass, flashlight, and kaleidoscope, for example, can provide useful observations as to how the child goes about the business of looking and seeing. Does he wish to share what he sees or does he prefer, instead, to keep his perceptions secret? These toys are also useful to our understanding of the child's views of big and little, near and far, dark and light—even his ideas about privacy or nighttime worries. We have known children who have used the flashlight to design elaborate stop-and-go scenarios, in this way showing us something about order and control in their lives and about those situations beyond their control.

Magnets, string, glue and scotch tape bring things together and are often the means through which children tell us of their worries and concerns about people leaving them, things getting lost, damaged and repaired. They often permit the child to show us how he tried to "put together" things which may not fit. Afterwards, these very same toys can be used by the same child to put things together more sensibly.

Fingerprints, clay, Silly Putty and the like all permit socially acceptable messing and pounding activities, although some therapists may prefer one over the others. This brings us to the idea that the child therapist should be comfortable with his toys, using only those which he knows well and with which he feels at ease.

Dolls, small animals and puppets lend themselves to eliciting ideas about the child's family and his experiences of protection or destruction. Often, animals and dolls allow the child to express affects, fears and concerns—sometimes even duplicating the tones of voice in which the child has been disciplined. Through this medium, the child can verbally relate attitudes, feelings and even specific words or injunctions of others, which he might be unable to convey without the toy.

The moving toys—cars, trucks, planes and boats—permit the child to recapture past events, separations from others, impending vacations, as well as his own experiences and style with motion, space and travel.

The playroom should have sufficient variety to allow children of differing ages, skills, sexes and styles to interact, communicate and also have a good time! Selection of toys inappropriate to a child's age—for example, offering dolls to a 12-year-old—can invite appropriate disdain. Small animals and dolls may suggest to such a child that the therapist or worker has scant respect for his interests and wishes. If, however, the 12-year-old chooses the dolls from varied offerings, this choice may tells us something about the child's vulnerability to regression.

An adequately supplied toy room or toy kit might include the following durable toys and games:

Several dolls	Glue	Books, appealing to
Small animals	String	various ages
Puppets	Clay or Silly Putty	Dart gun—for those
Clay	Cards	who feel comfortable
Crayons	Chess and/or checkers set	with it
Paint	Vehicles	Play money
Paper	Blocks or other building	Doctor kit
Scotch tape	toys	Nesting barrels

Again, unwrap the toys and get to know them. It is wise to have two of some toys in order to facilitate interaction and communication between the therapist and the child.

Since the playroom is a microcosm of the child's world and experience with his therapist, the constancy of that environment should be protected. A child may initially see and note a toy without choosing it, but, at some later time, decide to explore it. Other children become attached to specific toys whose disappearance may become worrisome. Although the child may not tell you directly, he may believe that the stability and value of important objects are underestimated or ignored. As some children become more skilled with a toy or game with which they play all the time, the therapist can observe their growing proficiency while the child gains the experience of mastery and effectiveness.

When a child chooses to paint or make something, it is useful to set aside a storage space which will convey the value of those productions as well as the continuity of the environment. Nevertheless, the child cannot expect that large productions will always be saved. Explain this simply and clearly. Sometimes a drawing or representation of the large work can be saved instead.

If a child makes a big mess and dumps toys everywhere, don't expect him to clean up. Janitorial services are not normally a part of the therapeutic contract; if they are an implicit part of yours, perhaps some renegotiation is in order.

If toys overstimulate the child and he becomes too excited, it is wise to help him control himself. The therapist can facilitate the reemergence of that control by limiting the available selection of toys, helping the child to slow down, and clearly affirming the simple rules of the interaction in the office. Sometimes, a novice worker will mistakenly believe that a child gains from "working out his aggression" through breaking and destroying objects. Rarely is this productive. On the contrary, such activity is overly stimulating, produces guilt, and renders empty our verbalizations that ours is a "safe place." Here, having a double "set of controls" (two of each toy) is especially helpful: The worker can suggest in action and speech how one might use these materials differently and, perhaps, more productively.

Holidays and birthdays are a tricky business. Whether to offer a gift or not should be as carefully and thoughtfully considered as its selection. To offer a gift implies considerable intimacy—that is, that you *really* know the recipient. You are not a benevolent aunt or uncle; however, your first impulse as a novice may be to give in order to establish that friendship from which the treatment will proceed. Sometimes, the child experiences this as a bribe which invites his compliance before he may be ready to trust. Very often the child needs friendly understanding much more than a gift. In any event, never give a gift from the playroom.

In playing a competitive game, novice therapists are often tempted to "throw" the game so the child will feel pleased about winning. Usually a child knows full well that adults can do more than he can and often he feels cheated when he becomes aware that he has been the winner of a spurious victory engineered for his "benefit." Furthermore, the purpose of our work is not to fabricate facile victories, but to help each child deal with his own experiences, including his realistic development limitations.

When a child cheats, however, it is important to observe this behavior without moralizing and lecturing. This can sometimes be accomplished quite directly by noting that the child has changed the rules because he seems so eager to win at all costs. To ignore his cheating out of a mistaken wish to be overly tactful fails to acknowledge that you are interested in the child and want to understand his wishes and feelings. Simultaneously, you are helping him achieve what he is able to accomplish at his level of skill. Conversely, you do not play chess with a child in a manner which conveys that winnings is tremendously important to your own self-esteem. The therapist is neither the architect of vacuous victories nor the stern personification of absolutes and unyielding "reality."

There are many lovely examples in the literature of therapeutic play interaction familiar even to novice workers, who (unfortunately—if understandably) tend to undervalue their own work in comparison with these vignettes of skillful, easily demonstrated therapeutic movement. It is worth remembering that work with a new patient will not necessarily crystallize into a picture of similar classical clarity. Be patient. Don't expect that your first efforts will at once produce new chapters on the theory and practice of helping troubled children. Instead, slow down enough to allow yourself a growing fascination with and respect for the minutiae of human behavior.

Beginners sometimes handicap themselves by attempting to fit the details of the child's play behavior to their own preoccupation with some grand concept. Even when such grand concepts are truly important, they may be superseded by an event in the child's life which is more pertinent at the moment. In any case, the readiness of the child to comprehend "the grand interpretation" must rest on the building blocks of repeated smaller observations and interpretations of the detailed behavior.

For example, nine-year-old Tony arrived for his hour with his second therapist looking somewhat morose. He found it difficult to settle on any particular toy or game, moving from one to the other, falling silent periodically and seeming to have little energy for the interchange. The therapist made various attempts to engage him in play, but failed to remark on Tony's sadness or to inquire about it. Tony finally began to draw a roadway and place various vehicles on it. He interrupted this play and inquired whether his therapist "will graduate and leave like Dr. Silversmith did." The therapist replied that he would graduate too, but not for a long time. There was further discussion about this issue and the drawing resumed. The picture became a treasure map and Tony commented that there were silver coins hidden. In his play, they were unearthed and, once exposed, quickly covered over again. The therapist, aware of Tony's conflict about keeping and exposing secrets, began a vigorous effort to interpret and explain this theme. In the preoccupation with the grand theme, which was a very real problem area, he had missed the specific connection between the silver coins, Dr. Silversmith and the sad mood.

Tony responded by increased irritability and withdrawal. Just before the session closed, Tony commented, "I lost a friend today." As the therapist later reported: "At that moment, I finally got it."

The foregoing example illustrates the importance of slowing down when you feel that you are beginning to understand the meaning of a child's play behavior. Your own understanding will probably precede the child's ability to cope with such ideas—much less accept your observations as his own. You may want to test, tentatively, these observations by asking the child for his "corrections" and his perspective; for example, "I think I'm beginning to catch on. . . ." or, "I see —maybe you're showing me that you get worried about this." To bombard him prematurely with your own perceptions grossly underestimates the importance, not only of the child's unique pattern of learning, but of his particular feelings stemming from some of the issues which arise.

FURTHER READING

Aries, P. (1962), *Centuries of Childhood: A Social History of Family Life*. New York: Knopf.
Erikson, Erik (1937), Configurations in Play. *Psychoanalytic Quarterly*, 6:139-214.
Erikson, Erik (1940), Studies in the Interpretation of Play. *Genetic Psychology Monographs*, 22:557-671.
Levin, Sidney and Werner, Henry (1966), The Significance of Giving Gifts to Children in Therapy. *Journal of the American Academy of Child Psychiatry*, 5:630-652.
Peller, Lili (1954), Libidinal Phases, Ego Development and Play. *Psychoanalytic Study of the Child*, 9:178-198.

III

CLINICAL BEGINNINGS

7

Diagnostic Assessments

In this chapter, various aspects of the "beginnings" of clinical work with children, adolescents, and their families are illustrated by sample cases.

The first of these "beginnings" concerns the diagnostic sessions with the child and the family who are requesting help for the first time. Such an evaluation must have as its aims:

1) *The setting in motion of the relationship between the therapist and the family.* This includes getting to know the family members, while they in turn are assessing for themselves whether they are welcomed, respected, understood and compatible with the therapist. Many cases flounder because the therapist, in his determination to secure necessary information, fails to recognize that this beginning process involves high levels of anxiety and uncertainty, as well as fear that judgment, rather than compassionate understanding, will be rendered. These beginning sessions give the family a sample of what this particular kind of help is like.

2) *The gathering of an adequate amount of information in order to develop a beginning idea of the nature, extent, onset and context of the difficulties which bring the parent to seek psychological help for the child.* The definition of an adequate amount of information is illusory and, therefore, the pacing and duration of the information-gathering process should be variable and dic-

tated by the particular families. Beginning therapists tend either to rush through this initial process, assuming that no therapy occurs until the evaluation is complete, or protract the information-gathering process endlessly, out of the mistaken view that total clarity is possible in this early phase.

3) *The development of a thoughtful but invariably tentative set of ideas about the people in the family, their difficulties, the possible origins of their problems and what assistance can be offered.*

4) *The conveying of these ideas back to the family.* This provides them with an opportunity to test whether these ideas and suggestions are reasonable and understandable. When such a process is mutual, the final aim of the diagnostic evaluation has been served, namely, helping the family decide upon the appropriate next steps. If that decision is for further treatment, this is what is commonly referred to as the contracting process. It has been our experience that the consumers of psychiatric services have justifiably complained about being less than full participants in the contractual process. This step should never be skipped nor should treatment be dictated without the family's understanding and cooperation.

Typically a diagnostic evaluation consists of the following events:

1) one or more interviews with the parents;
2) one or more interviews/play sessions with the child;
3) selective gathering of information from other sources, such as schools, physicians and/or social agencies;
4) time for thinking about and organizing the information, usually in a written account;
5) the post-diagnostic reporting to the family.

In organizing the write-up of an evaluation, the following categories may be a useful framework.

I. *Identifying data*
   A. Ages of child, parents, sibs and others in household.
   B. A description of the family's realities: housing, economics, school, health, etc.

    C. Dates and number of visits with each person seen, including cancellations.

II. *Presenting Complaints*

    A. The nature and history of the child's difficulties.

    B. Other agencies or persons involved in the referral, and their concerns.

III. *Description of the Parents*

    A. General description of parents and their interactions with each other, with the child, and with the therapist.

    B. Attitude toward problems of the child, and their ideas about etiology.

IV. *Relevant Family History*

    A. Singificant events in parents' lives.

    B. Selective inquiry about the parents' experience as children.

    C. Significant events in lives of family members.

V. *Developmental History*

    A. A sequential account of the child's development.

    B. Significant stresses and their impact on the child's developmental progress.

VI. *Interviews with Child*

    A. Description of child, including physical appearance, manner, affect, shifts in behavior, etc.

    B. Concise description of the flow of each hour.

VII. *Dynamic Formulation and Diagnosis*

    A. Integration of all relevant data into a coherent statement of the major forces at work currently and etiologically.

    B. Description of areas which remain unclear and need further clarification.

VIII. *Recommendations*

    A. Regarding direct work with the child; frequency and treatment modalities.

B. Regarding direct work with others in the immediate family. Most typically this means work with parents; however other significant people may be included.
C. Regarding possible environmental changes for the family's benefit (e.g., school placement, tutoring, etc.).
D. Regarding further evaluation procedures, such as psychological or other tests, neurological examinations, etc.

Four examples of diagnostic evaluations follow, each of which leads to different formulations and recommendations.

CASE 1—MARK ROSS

Mark Ross is a four-year-old white male, the only child of Mrs. Jean Ross, a former nurse, age 27, and Morton Ross, a law student, age 29. The Rosses have been married for five years. They were referred to the clinic by one of Mr. Ross' law professors because of their concern with Mark's sleep problems. In the course of the workup, I had two joint sessions with both parents, one session with each parent separately, and two play sessions with Mark.

Presenting Complaint

About a month before the Ross' first contact with the clinic, Mark began to have trouble sleeping. At that time he told his parents he saw a ghost standing by his bed, and since then he had trouble going to sleep. Typically, he would come into his parents' bedroom and sleep on a pallet on the floor. The parents connect the onset of these symptoms with their having taken him to see "Earthquake," a film in which he saw people crushed and drowned. Since then, a time which coincided with his mother's quitting work because of illness, Mark has been asking about people and things dying; he worries, particularly, about his mother.

Current Circumstances

In February, Mrs. Ross quit her job as a nurse because of recurrent *petit mal* seizures, including one in which she blacked out and knocked over a drink at an office party. She became increasingly concerned about making an error in caring for the patients and felt the job had become too much of a challenge. She reported feeling inadequate, incompetent and fearful that her blackouts would lead her to make critical mistakes. Because her nursing job was a major source of their income (Mr. Ross had two more years to go in law school), they felt they could no longer afford to send Mark to the nursery school, which he had attended daily from nine to five for six months. He had been in another nursery school since age two-and-one-half. As a result of his mother's illness, Mark's entire life pattern has totally changed. From a full day of planned activities with other children, he has gone to a day at home, alone with a mother identified as "too sick to work"; she, in turn, has gone from a demanding full-time job to being home with a great deal of time on her hands and a young child on whom to focus exclusively. She has not spent this much time at home since Mark was six months old, at which time she went back to school for her nurse's training. In addition, there have been increasing tensions between the parents.

History

Mark was an unplanned baby, born a year after the Rosses married. "We originally did want two children," Mrs. Ross reported, "but not so soon." Now, with increased financial and marital stress, they are no longer thinking of having a second child. Mark was a full-term baby and weighed 7 lbs. 15 oz. at birth. According to the mother, the pregnancy and delivery were uncomplicated. However, Mark was born with a defect of his penis, hypospadias.

He was described as a "good baby," who presented no special feeding or sleeping problems. He was bottle-fed and Mrs. Ross does not remember exactly when he was weaned to a cup. When he was about six months old, Mrs. Ross began school and was gone most of the day. At that time, and for two subsequent years, Mr. Ross was an officer in the Navy. They reported that Mark, as an infant, was taken with them everywhere—to friends' houses in the evenings, etc. When Mark was 18 months old, Mr. Ross was sent overseas for a year. Mrs. Ross and Mark remained in this country while she continued to attend nursing school.

At about age three, six months after his father returned, Mark had surgery for the hypospadias. He may require another cosmetic operation. The parents said that he was a very good patient. They spent a great deal of time with him during his hospital stay. He did not require complicated post-operative care, although he did have an indwelling catheter while in the hospital.

The mother cannot remember exactly when Mark was toilet trained—"It just didn't seem that important." But she thought the toileting went smoothly, and by age two-and-one-half to three, he was fully trained. The only previous sleep disturbance she recalled was around age two-and-one-half, when the father returned from overseas. This disturbance was apparently short-lived.

Parents' Description of Child

The parents reported that Mark is "hyperactive," "outgoing," and has no problems with separation. Recently, he has been more aggressive and manipulative with other children. According to the mother, he uses "I love you" and "I hate you" as ways to get what he wants. He knows that his mother takes medicine and has recently expressed concern about the death of trees, flowers and his parents. He was described as loving, easily frustrated, and perfectionist. As an illustration the parents mentioned that he must get his socks on perfectly straight or he will get annoyed—a trait the father appeared to recognize in himself.

This view of Mark was consistent with the report of Mark's nursery school teacher, who told me that he was incredibly active, a real leader among the children, very bright and restless, but with the capacity to concentrate when interested. She agreed that Mark was manipulative in the sense of using tears to get what he wants.

Observation Sessions with Mark (One week apart)

Mark was an engaging, good-looking child, with a Buster Brown haircut. He was slim but sturdy and missing a front tooth. The tooth was knocked out at age three while he was roughhousing with his father. The father described it as a "traumatic" experience for both of them and said that Mark urged him to "put the tooth back." In both of our sessions, he was neatly dressed in jeans, polo shirt, and cowboy boots. In session 1, he came willingly enough but made a trip to the waiting room midway "to see if Mommy's still there. I'll be right back." He appeared alert, active and curious, and his behavior toward me was directed toward using me as a helper—getting me to help him use the gun, get down the darts, etc. He spent most of the first hour playing with the toy gun and darts. He discovered that if he shot them on to the overhead light fixture, they made a satisfying sound and clung there more tenaciously before dropping than if he shot them against the walls. He showed much pleasure when the darts fell, excitedly reloading the gun—a maneuver he worked out by holding the gun between his legs and using both hands to push down the quite heavy spring. This play went on for about 35 minutes of the hour, and was interspersed with attention to other toys, particularly the doctor's kit and the stethoscope.

He told me he was coming here in order "to meet you," and he added, somewhat cryptically, "I know everyone here . . . ." He also told me that he had had a gun at home, but he broke it. When I asked how that had happened, he said he didn't know but he'd get another one from Santa Claus. Near the end of the session he put down the gun and drew a boy—a head, two legs and two eyes. As I asked him some questions about the boy, he drew in a mouth. In response to my queries, he told me the boy's name was Charley, he was four, he liked playing with his toys and guns, and he didn't like to color. Then he said, "Write—A boy—he's mad at this" (shooting the gun at the wall); "he's afraid—of loud noises; he's sad—about crying."

In this first session, Mark gave no indication of gross disturbance or thought disorder. He had a good capacity to attend and persist. Mark's affect was animated but not uncontrolled. He handled play materials dexterously, and he did not seem particularly anxious about separating. I wondered about the strong preoccupation with gun play. This play might be overdetermined because Mrs. Ross had forbidden him to have guns in the past, had bought him one several days earlier, had withheld it from him for a while as a punishment, had then let him sleep with it in a holster on the bed (and noted that this was the first night in which he did not ask to come into the parents' bed). The next day he told her he had broken it. She reported that, after he broke the gun, he asked, "Are you happy?"

Session 2 served to confirm most of these impressions of a reasonably well-integrated and active child, except that he appeared somewhat more concerned about being separated from the mother. Some of this increased anxiety may have been due to the death, several days earlier, of his great grandfather—Mrs. Ross' grandfather, of whom she was very fond. In any case, this time he made three trips to the waiting room, to get a drink and also to check on his mother's presence. The gun play continued but less intently and with a rather creative elaboration. Mark found that if he stuck the suction ends of the darts together he could use the two as a longer projectile. In fact, several "linking" themes emerged in this session. Mark seemed to be working on the problem of making connections—between the two darts, between a toy car and a trailer, between himself and mother-in-the-waiting-room, and between himself and the lost but remembered world of nursery school. Thus, he spent the bulk of the hour working on a drawing of a boy—this time with arms and rudimentary hands, as well as the head and legs of the earlier drawing—which he said was a letter to his erstwhile nursery school friend, John. He then elaborately covered the drawing with paste, folded the paste-covered drawing many times and carefully sealed it, like a letter. The most noteworthy feature of the pasting behavior was his desire to use his fingers and his fear of getting his hands sticky. He made repeated requests for "a napkin" to wipe off his sticky fingers and finally decided he preferred applying the paste with the applicator. It should be noted that the nursery school teacher did not feel that concern about messing had been a prominent feature in his school play.

Mark also expressed some concern about food and eating ("Do you eat lunch here? Do you have any candy? You have to buy some."). Some of these questions may have been ways to link my office with the nursery school setting, putting it into a more known and hence manageable context, in which playing, eating lunch, etc., are part of the regular routine.

Again, I did not feel that Mark's behavior was conspicuously disturbed or out of the range of the four-year-old children I have observed over the years in nursery school settings.

Impressions of Parents and Parental Interactions
(Based on two joint sessions and one session
with each parent alone)

Mrs. Ross seemed to be a depressed, fearful woman, with a damped-down affect and a kind of simpleness or vacancy—periods when she almost literally seemed to be "not quite there." Physically, she is short, has long brown hair and a pleasant face with a somewhat mask-like appearance. Her epilepsy was diagnosed from slight blackouts and EEG evidence at age 16, but she said that she didn't believe the diagnosis until she had had her first *grand mal* seizure in her late teens. She has been on substantial dosages of Dilantin and phenobarbital ever since, and the dosages have been increased since the last seizure prompted her quitting work. The pills make her drowsy. She said that she was afraid of working as a nurse, where life-and-death decisions are involved, and as the tension mounted and slight seizures increased, she had quit her job. With her permission, I contacted her neurologist, who reported that she should not be driving and that she should be followed closely.

Four weeks after the initial joint interview, Mrs. Ross reported that Mark's problem had abated considerably. He was sleeping much better, and when he did awake in the middle of the night, if she just said, "We're here," he went back to sleep.

Thus, she now saw the focus of difficulty as the tensions she and her husband had been having. Mrs. Ross felt that her husband was not "emotional enough," and she said that when she asked, "Do you love me?" he answered, "I don't know." He defined her love for him in terms of doing the dishes and keeping the house neat, and she was not very committed to housework. She reported that he didn't think she was pretty, that he didn't respond to her overtures, and that they had only had sexual relations a few times in the past year, partly because he was always tense and tired from his heavy school obligations. She reported that he also watched her anxiously when they went out for fear she would have a seizure, and this watchfulness disturbed her. The only happy times she recalled were during the first few months of the marriage, before she became pregnant, and immediately after Mr. Ross returned from overseas.

She claimed that she liked being home, but appeared hard put to plan activities for Mark that would make up for the stimulation of nursery school. Her efforts to find a free or low-cost nursery school had been unsuccessful. She felt that part of the reason for Mark's improvement was that she was now paying more attention to him.

Mr. Ross was a tall, bearded man with longish brown hair beginning to recede in front, gold-rimmed glasses, and a rather immobile face. His affect, too, was flat—not so much depressed, somehow, as controlled and armored. He spoke fairly precisely and had an obsessive need to know just what was expected of him. He was the second son of a "conservative" family. In my session alone with him, he rephrased most of my questions, saying, "You mean such-and-such?" He was vague about most feelings and had trouble describing relationships. He mentioned that he and his wife had "trouble communicating"—but gave no details. Yet, in one of the joint sessions, it was he who corrected his wife about her feelings on learning about Mark's birth defect. She reported being "surprised," and he said, "You were very upset, don't you remember? I was too and I wondered if it would interfere with his sex life and how he'd feel comparing his penis with other boys' when he was an adolescent." His manner toward his wife was distinctly condescending, despite a surface show of being democratic. Something about their interaction suggested that she could be easily "gaslighted" into believing she was more incompetent than she actually was.

However, in the session with me alone, Mr. Ross said that he reassured his wife about her epilepsy, encouraging her not to think of herself as defective by pointing out that if it were such a handicap, they wouldn't have let her work as a nurse in her various jobs. He believed that she could "will her spells" and that she induced them by thinking about them. He suggested that she wanted *him* to make the decision for her to quit work by bringing home nightly stories of the day's traumas. He said, "I don't hold it against her," in a way that made me suspect that he may resent her leaving her work. He added that even at home Mrs. Ross created pressures for herself. He also said that he tried to "bring her back" when he noticed her staring and was hurt and annoyed that she seemed angry at his efforts to do so.

This kind of blaming fit with Mrs. Ross' readiness to accept blame. Mr. Ross said the main problem of the marriage was "we're not that close—there's a lack of communication." Talking about their sexual problem, he attributed the distance in part to her falling asleep earlier than he goes to bed. Recalling their years together, he thought that the only time they were really close was during their courtship. He only knew her a few months, was drawn to her "because she liked to do what I liked to do—swimming, going to beaches; we worked in the same place, and I liked her family." He also said that he got married because "he was running scared," but did not elaborate except to say that he felt that being out of college, he should get married. He thought things began going downhill after Mark was born, though he didn't regret the timing of Mark's birth. He didn't worry much about the epilepsy, thinking that since there was no other history of it in Mrs. Ross' family, it was probably "just a mutation." He seemed to see his wife as a defective person who could lose control at any time. Mr. Ross spoke with almost no variation of affect. He often sat with his hand across his crotch. He had great difficulty in talking about feelings. The only change in emotional tone which I noted was when he began talking about Mark. "I love him," he said, and broke into a smile. It was for Mark that he thought of keeping the marriage together. He wondered if that were sufficient justification and didn't know if there were enough left between his wife and him to salvage the marriage. He said that he was willing to try if it didn't cost too much money or take too much time. He also reported that Mark was much better. He explained the improvement as follows: "He's gotten used to the idea that he doesn't go to nursery school anymore; he stays home with mother."

Summary and Recommendations

The problem in the Ross family appears to represent a parental crisis overlaid on some typical issues and conflicts at this time in Mark's development. The mother and father are both remote people. While this type of character problem appears to be long-standing in both parents, it seems to have been exacerbated by the mother's recently increased sense of professional and personal inadequacy, her increased tensions about her epilepsy leading to her retirement from nursing, her feelings of uncertainty about mothering, the tension to which Mr. Ross is subjected as a full-time law student with a minimal income, and the gradually growing dissatisfaction both partners have experienced with the marriage.

The mother is not only depressed and guilty, she is pharmacologically slowed down as well. Indeed, it is hard to distinguish between the possible effects of the medication used in managing her epilepsy and the effects of her depressive and masochistic personality. The father is also relatively unavailable much of the time, although he does make greater efforts to reach out to the child than he does to engage his wife.

The increased parental tension is accompanied by a nearly total reversal in Mark's world: He has gone from a crowded, stimulating day lasting from nine to five and filled with play materials, teachers, and other children to a relatively empty schedule at home, with no other children around, and with a mother who appears to be "out of it" a good bit of the time.

Although Mark shows some anxiety and some potential for compulsive behavior, these do not seem at present to be damaging or to warrant psychotherapeutic intervention. It would be well to keep in mind, however, that from Mark's history, one could expect a heightened potential for difficulties in terms of his castration anxiety (i.e., the hypospadias defect, the initial operative procedure, the possibility of another such operation in the future; the loss of a tooth at age three). It may be that his gun play—handling, shooting, putting the gun between his legs—reflects this preoccupation. Oedipal concerns seem to be reflected in his anxiety about sleeping separately from the parents. These concerns should be kept in mind in future planning and assessment of Mark's progress. At this point, however, the treatment of choice would seem to be environmental changes, to assure a more stimulating world, and therapy for the parents.

1) It is recommended that Mark be given additional opportunity for enrichment of his daily environment—whether through summer school, nursery program, or other available resources. The director of his nursery school told me that some kind of scholarship or part-time program might be worked out for Mark if his parents were in-

terested. Some attempt might also be made to reopen Mark's contacts with his nursery school playmates.

2) Conjoint therapy is recommended for the parents around issues of child rearing and especially around their own deteriorated relationship. If it seemed a useful option in the course of the conjoint therapy, either or both of the parents might be encouraged to try individual therapy as well.

Post-Diagnostic Session with Parents

I met with the Rosses and discussed recommendations with them. They were relieved to hear that therapy was not recommended for Mark at this time and said that they will follow up on a nursery school for him.

They were receptive to conjoint therapy and I told them that they would hear from someone in the clinic about this soon.

Discussion

The evaluation of his family and of Mark in particular illustrates a variety of heightened family pressures. These disrupted Mark's entire living pattern on the one hand and heightened the normative concerns of this developmental stage. Paradoxically, the mother's full-time presence at home—precipitated by her appropriate concern about the relationship between her illness and her job responsibilities —intensified Mark's worries about separation and aggression.

The two play sessions demonstrate Mark's awareness of the conflicts eddying about him. The sessions also suggest some levels of internal conflict but these are far outweighed by his intactness, his sturdiness and his competence.

We can reasonably speculate about the emergence of the night terrors and why they receded. Such transient symptoms are not unusual in children at this age. Because of their own difficulties, Mr. and Mrs. Ross were unable to provide the understanding and firmness which normally help children manage such fears. In addition, the abrupt changes in his familiar life-pattern served to intensify the underlying anxieties.

During the evaluation several factors may have contributed to the reparative work. Firstly, Mark was given the opportunity for more direct expression of aggressive impulses through the gun play in the play sessions and through his mother's permission to have the heretofore forbidden toy at home. It is likely that these opportunities relieved some anxiety about the acceptability of aggressive wishes and about his ability to express, control and master them.

Furthermore, the parents' diminished concern about the night terrors and their handling of them probably enhanced Mark's sense of safety. It is also likely that the parents' attention to their own marital difficulties placed the "problem" in the family into a more appropriate perspective.

Thus, we can see the symptoms recede in the course of the evaluation, although fragments of separation concerns persist and the evaluator appropriately points to possible future problems. Although these are sensible, tentative predictions based on his history, the recent stresses and the continuing marital problems, such predictions can only be tested over time. The readiness of the parents to be seen in conjoint therapy will provide the opportunity to reassess Mark should further difficulties emerge.

The advice given to enrich Mark's daily activities and the help given to implement this advice are entirely reasonable. One would hope that the conjoint therapy might also aim to enrich the mother's daily activities through investigation of other occupational directions.

The recommendations and the proposed treatment plan not only aim to repair problems but address the issue of continuing developmental progress for all members of this family.

CASE 2—ALICIA THOMAS

Identifying Information

Alicia Thomas is a nine-year-old, black, fourth grader. She is the fifth of eight children in an intact family.

Referral

Alicia was referred by her physician one year ago. She was being treated for a duodenal ulcer, which is very unusual at her age. Apparently, her parents have waited until now to act on this referral.

Presenting Complaints

Alicia developed symptoms of continuous vomiting and abdominal pain about 14 months ago. Extensive tests revealed that she had a peptic ulcer. Since then, she has been hospitalized four times. She had had almost continuous gastrointestinal symptoms, including intermittent pain and periods of vomiting, often in the morning. As a result of this, she has missed about a third of her total school days. According to Mr. and Mrs. Thomas, none of these episodes has been related to external stress; however, characteristically they do not make such connections. There is no history of symptoms prior to 14 months ago. The pediatrician raised the question about whether the parents might have overlooked developing symptoms until they became unavoidable.

The mother reported that Alicia has had vomiting periods on the average of once or twice a month ever since birth. They have always been explained as "viruses." Also, Alicia has always had a tendency to get carsick. Most of the time, she was not taken to a pediatrician for these symptoms.

Alicia's reaction to hospital was noteworthy. She enjoyed being in the hospital and was reluctant to go home each time. The development of the ulcer symptoms was soon followed by the development of many fears, including disturbing nightmares in which people were usually killed or dismembered. Very often she related these to the death of her brother, Tim, and fears about other deaths in the family. Frequently, Alicia would go to bed at night worrying that somebody would be killed during the evening. When her parents went out, Alicia stayed up, waiting for them to come home; she then told them that she was worried that they would get hurt or killed. She told her parents about her fears in great detail. Often, in the middle of the night, she came into her parents' room and attempted to sleep in the bed with them. Recently Alicia has been sleeping in her sister's bed. The parents reported that these terrors have increased considerably over the past month and Alicia is now refusing to take the yearly family trip to Disneyland because she is afraid to fly.

Developmental History

Birth. None of the children in the Thomas family were planned, but the mother stated that they were all wanted. Alicia's birth was one of the hardest. The mother was continuously sick toward the end of the pregnancy and suffered from fluid retention and hypertension. Since these symptoms were similar to those that had accompanied the pregnancy with a prior child who was born mentally and physically defective, Mrs. Thomas worried quite a bit during the latter part of this pregnancy. She reported that, after delivery, she was depressed for about two months. Although postpartum depression was not unusual for her, she recalled that this was the worst.

Landmarks. As far as Mrs. Thomas remembered, Alicia was not an unusual baby except for her vomiting. The motor development was apparently normal. Her speech development was reported as precocious. Although the mother and father do not remember the details, they recalled that Alicia surprised everybody by being able to say sentences at a very early age.

Events. Apparently, until about age five, everything went pretty smoothly. The events of note during years one through five include a hospitalization for two weeks for croup at age one. Her brother was sent to a state hospital for the mentally retarded sometime before her first birthday. Alicia knew her brother and visited him often. Mrs. Thomas started to work as a clerk shortly after Alicia was born. She left Alicia in the care of her niece. Five years ago, she changed to part-time work.

When Alicia was between the ages of five and seven, a series of traumatic events occurred. Mr. Thomas had a serious accident and was unable to work for four years thereafter. He was hospitalized several times, once for back surgery. Alicia's brother died at the state hospital around the same time. The mother did not notice much of a reaction to the brother's death. Six months later, an older brother was killed in a car crash. Alicia reacted somewhat more to this and asked "a lot of questions," particularly about why the other boy in the car didn't die. At age seven, Alicia's maternal grandmother, who lived with the family, was hospitalized for two months following a stroke.

Alicia's symptoms began just before her eighth birthday. Six months later, her father returned to work as a salesman. His late hours disturbed Alicia, since he had formerly spent much time with the children.

Routines. Alicia has always been a picky eater, something the mother states is true of all the children. Although there have been periodic sleep disturbances, the current problems are far more intense and persistent. Sleeping arrangements in the home shift periodically; the children often change and share beds. Several months prior to the evaluation, Alicia preferred to sleep with her baby sister; during the past month, she has slept with her oldest sister.

Alicia has friends and is reported to like school. Her teacher, however, notes that Alicia is a perfectionist and gets upset when she doesn't do well, requiring a great deal of reassurance.

The Family. There is a strong sense of kinship in this family. The one married son lives across the street. The youngster killed in the car accident often provided care for his younger sibs. The retarded son was visited very frequently by the entire family until his death.

The father's accident and his subsequent inability to work were clearly a source of great distress to him. He described feeling incompetent and attempted to compensate by working at "odd jobs" and participating in community affairs. For example, he was a member of the Parents' Association at Alicia's school. He reported that he became more strict following his accident and developed many physical symptoms, one of which was erroneously thought to be a peptic ulcer. During this stressful period, he was in psychiatric treatment for some six to eight months.

Parents' History

Mr. and Mrs. Thomas have been married for 30 years. They met when they were in high school. There have been several stormy periods during their marriage. Usually the issue has been the father's ambition. Mrs. Thomas complained that he devoted too little time to the family.

Mr. Thomas is the seventh child of ten and the oldest male in his family. His father owned a farm and a funeral home. Mr. Thomas was required to assume a lot of responsibility for his family early and was somewhat resentful that this precluded a good education. He graduated from high school. He has worked as an auto mechanic for most of his life, and at the time of his accident was a part owner of a service station. After the accident, he was forced to give up his business and has lived mainly on Social Security, his wife's income, and loans from other members of his family. Presently, he works as a salesman from 9 a.m. until 9 p.m.

Mrs. Thomas was an only child. Her mother died in childbirth and she was raised by her grandmother. Her father lived in the same town and apparently saw her several times a week. She remembered her childhood as pleasant.

Mr. and Mrs. Thomas were married when he was 18 and she 16. They moved from their hometown to the Bay Area in 1950.

Interviews: Alicia

Interview #1. Alicia made herself comfortable at once and talked easily throughout the hour. She told story after story of fears and worries, portraying herself as the helpless victim. There was far less feeling expressed than one would expect from the dramatic content of the stories. She would frequently assume the posture of someone thinking very hard about what she was saying.

With little prompting, she spoke of a dream she had the previous night, in which she and her sister were mangled in a train wreck. This was followed by the memory of a dream when she was six, in which she saw a man with a knife in his head. She wasn't sure if this was real or not. Once she thought she might actually be dead. She worries always that she, or someone else in the family, may die. Particularly when her parents go out at night, she worries they will die and not return. She told me these fears. had gotten worse since her brothers died.

She talked about her ulcer and called it a continuous "stomach pain" and "sometimes even a head pain." Ulcers are "sores in your stomach"—sometimes they hurt "inside" and sometimes "outside."

She said she was coming to see me to have the "fears taken out of her head." However, at first she thought I might actually "shrink heads." These reports had a dramatic quality. When I asked whether her parents helped her with her worries, she said "they did, but not enough." She always goes to them, but their reassurance is not terribly helpful and "they don't spend enough time with me."

Interview #2. Alicia immediately told me that I had helped her a great deal in our last interview. She wasn't afraid for a few days and didn't have as many nightmares. She said I had done this for her by understanding her. She remembered my exact words: "It must be hard to have those worries." She wished her mother would do that. She told me that not only her mother and her father, but her brothers and sisters didn't really have enough time for her. Rather than play with her they preferred to watch "horror stories." She would rather play games with them, for instance a game callled "who is the best and prettiest." At the end of the hour, she confided that she had no best friends in school like the other kids and that this was "a big problem."

She was eager to talk and played only with some encouragement from me. She built a "flying car" out of tinker toys and told a simple story that this car had big radio antennae and got "good music" so that people who owned it could have lots of friends.

Interview with Parents

Mrs. Thomas is larger and taller than her husband and dominated our interview both physically and verbally.

My impression of Mr. Thomas was of a man who was always trying hard to do the right thing. He focused extensively on his achievements, for instance, his work on the school board, and stated repeatedly that Alicia and his family were proud of him. Despite this, he seemed rather pathetic and depressed.

Mrs. Thomas was very agreeable but independent and self-willed. She tended to run our interviews and corrected her husband on many occasions. It was clear that she was more aware than Mr. Thomas of family history, but both parents were somewhat vague.

The family has been severely shaken by the father's four years of illness and by their children's deaths. Both parents seem to be proud people, with high standards for themselves as well as for their children. They suggested that they are rather strict disciplinarians, expecting the children to behave as young adults. They seem to attend more to the children's behavior than to their emotional needs. An example of this was given by both Alicia and her father. Alicia's dog contracted an illness about a month before the evaluation. The father had taken the dog to the A.S.P.C.A., where he was told that the treatment would be very expensive. Without consulting Alicia, the father decided to have the dog "put to sleep." However, he had not told Alicia that he had made this decision by the time she came for the evaluation. During the evaluation, Alicia mentioned that the dog had disappeared several weeks before and that she had the suspicion that her father had had the dog "put to sleep," but that she was frightened to ask him about this.

The therapist conducting the evaluation had the impression that Mr. and Mrs. Thomas would support Alicia's treatment in spite of their earlier denial of Alicia's symptoms. They both said that they had become more aware of her emotional difficulties during the evaluation. The father said that he felt treatment would help "recover her great potential," which he feared would be lost as a result of her problems. The mother agreed that treatment could help.

Formulation

Alicia seems to be a bright, verbal child struggling with many fears. In addition to the ulcer, she has nightmares, and many phobias about death and mutilation.

The history and the clinical interviews suggest that Alicia experiences all impulses—neediness and assertiveness—as highly unacceptable and conflicted. While she can assert that she would like others to be more attentive, giving and protective, these statements are offset by her precocious style, her constricted affect and her too-quick efforts to please and comply. The intense internalized conflicts about impulse expression find their outlet in somatic and phobic symptoms. These permit regressions which are more acceptable to her and her family; "sick" appears more acceptable than "naughty," terror is more acceptable than demands for affection and supplies. The incident with Alicia's sick dog suggests that questions and discussion are often forbidden, while sickness itself can lead to death and loss. Her place in the middle of a large sibship and the family's economic hardships may also contribute to her sense that supplies—emotional and economic—are inadequate.

The real stresses within this family have perhaps reinforced Alicia's symptom "choice." Two brothers have died and the father has been seriously ill. A beloved grandmother has also been seriously ill. All these events occurred between the ages of five and seven, a developmental period when one would expect a child to begin to move away from dependence upon the family toward a sense of initiative and autonomy. Alicia must have experienced that taking this developmental thrust would be too dangerous and risk catastrophe. It is of some interest that she reports that she does not have a best friend, like some children do.

It is noteworthy that this child has no learning difficulties and is able to play with others her own age. While her symptoms are serious, her disturbance has not pervaded all areas of ego functioning. She is appealing, intact and able to work psychologically. This picture supports a tentative diagnosis of a neurotic child, actively struggling with her conflicts.

Summary of Psychological Testing

The psychological tests confirm the clinical impression of a bright, intact, neurotic child whose conflicts revolve around issues of neediness, aggression and sibling rivalry. Her response to these has been the development of a highly constricted defensive system which wards off the experience and expression of conflicted impulses. The internalized prohibition of impulse expression results in her flattened affect and tight control and leaves the symptoms as the only outlet.

Recommendations

The profound and alarming nature of Alicia's symptoms points to the need for immediate and intensive psychotherapeutic treatment. Her intelligence, verbal abilities, capacity to form a working relationship with the evaluator and her many areas of good functioning suggest that she can make good use of psychotherapy. She knows she needs help and is actively seeking it. While this comes across as too facile, her motivation is strong.

While the family remains under considerable stress and the parents will need help in experiencing and attending to Alicia's emotional needs, they are aware of her need for help and are committed to following through with it.

In sum, Alicia should begin intensive (probably more than once weekly) individual psychotherapy as soon as possible. Mr. and Mrs. Thomas should be seen by Alicia's therapist in regular, conjoint visits aimed at assisting them in understanding Alicia's problems and in examining ways in which they might respond to her needs.

Post-Diagnostic Interview with Mr. and Mrs. Thomas

Alicia's parents accepted the recommendations and expect to be contacted by a therapist in the immediate future.

Discussion

This assessment appears to be a thorough one, exploring the family situation, the history of the problem and Alicia's development, with particular attention to the stresses which preceded symptom formation. One gets a good sense of Alicia's strengths as well as her difficulties. Cognitive, affective, interpersonal and stress factors were explored, while adequate attention was also given to the family picture.

While the evaluator was able to form a fairly clear impression from his interviews, he remained uncertain about the possibility of a more severe disturbance. His concern about possible psychotic processes led to a request for psychological testing. We think that such a request was justified in light of the child's serious and early somatic problem. In addition, the child's dramatic presentation of intense fears and her rather rapid attachment to the therapist raised the appropriate question of differential diagnosis between a neurotic disturbance, with a predominantly hysterical quality, and an incipient psychotic or borderline process.

While the diagnostic process yields a beginning formulation about which we can be fairly confident, many questions remain to be clarified as treatment progresses. The parents' decision to seek an evaluation and their acceptance of the treatment recommendations remain puzzling in view of their earlier resistance and denial of the severity of Alicia's physical symptoms. It is possible that the father's recent return to work may have helped this family seek out assistance for Alicia now. It is frequently the case that people are able to seek psychological help for their children when other family problems are beginning to ease.

CASE 3—PAUL DUMONT

Identification

Paul Dumont is a 12-year-old, black, sixth grader who lives with his mother, four brothers, and his older sister and her two young children. He attends public school and is currently enrolled in a class for educationally handicapped children.

Presenting Complaint

The mother originally came on the advice of the school social worker because of numerous concerns expressed by his teacher about Paul's behavior. Although the mother did not feel anything was wrong with Paul, she was able to enumerate the reasons the school was upset. She told me that his teacher said that Paul generally plays alone, stares out of the window, ignores his class assignments, leaves the room frequently to sit or play in the hall, and, at times, does unusual things in class. He sometimes sits under a desk with his head covered or stands on his head in a closet. The mother also said that his teacher, Miss Lane, was disturbed by his eating habits, i.e., no breakfast at home and no school lunch.

Mrs. Dumont made an obvious effort to differentiate her opinion from the school's. She did not notice unusual things at home. She feels he has been a "loner" all his life. None of her children eats breakfast. Her main motivation was to please the school and "to find out for sure." Somewhat reservedly, she said that perhaps the school knows more, but her suspiciousness with regard to the school was obvious.

Development and Family Background

Paul is the second youngest child in a family of six. He has older brothers aged 13, 15 and 16, an older sister aged 19, and a younger brother who is 11. All the siblings, except his sister, are attending school.

The patient was born in Indianapolis, Indiana and lived there until age 10, at which time the entire family moved to California. Mrs. Dumont gave rapid, decisive answers regarding Paul's development. The pregnancy and birth were "normal." He was bottle- and breast-fed until the age of one. From six weeks of age, he had a baby-sitter during the day; Mrs. Dumont would breast-feed him after work. She could not remember any feeding problems but did say that he has never been a big eater. The mother proudly informed me that it was a family tradition to teach the children to fend for themselves early in life. In this regard, she noted that he ate by himself near one, walked by seven months and talked by nine months. He apparently reached developmental milestones around the same age as her other children, and he was never a worry to her. She recalled that Paul was toilet-trained by 18 months without assistance or direction. He has never had a problem with enuresis or encopresis. The parents separated when Paul was three or four. Little was said about Paul's father and their relationship, although the father lives in the area and visits the children weekly. No current sleep disturbance was reported, but Mrs. Dumont remembered that he "saw things" and was fearful at night at age three. This was not unusual for her children.

Paul has had two hospitalizations—bronchopneumonia that required three days in the hospital when he was three, and a more recent one 10 months ago for barbiturate overdose. This second hospitalization remains mysterious. One afternoon last October, Mrs. Dumont found him in a stuporous state and, subsequently, brought him to the hospital emergency room. A series of tests showed high barbiturate levels. When Paul was questioned, he was convinced that a cupcake he purchased at school had been drugged. The mother accepted this explanation and told me that none of her children has been involved with drugs.

Mrs. Dumont told me that Paul is interested in model cars, puzzles, and sports and generally plays peacefully by himself at home. He has always enjoyed his pets and, in recent years, he has had two or three dogs, rabbits, and two cats.

She sees nothing unusual in his relationships with his sibs. He fights with his brothers on occasion and generally plays with his own friends after school and on weekends. His most positive feelings are expressed toward his sister's two children, Maurice and Margaret.

Mrs. Dumont said that he was placed in an academically handicapped class beginning in the second grade. She told me that Paul was seen briefly by a school psychologist when he was in the fourth grade. She only talked with the therapist by phone. The school felt that he needed counseling because he would *only* use black crayons. She neither explored it further nor objected and, consequently, she knows very little about what transpired. It seems that he attended a special class from the second to the fourth grade and then entered regular classes just before leaving Indiana. Apparently, the separation from friends in Indiana was difficult for the whole family. No one wanted to leave. Mrs. Dumont's father was ill and she was needed here. Paul was upset about leaving a dog behind and disappointed about leaving old friends.

Interviews with Mrs. Dumont

Mrs. Dumont was a difficult woman to interview, initially, due to her defensiveness and overt hostility toward the school for their persistent efforts at recommending an evaluation. At first, she vigorously denied that anything was wrong with Paul but later acknowledged that he was "sensitive."

Initially, she sat stiffly in her chair, gave short, brief answers, rarely smiled, and blamed the school for not living up to their teaching responsibilities. Her suspiciousness of teachers extended to professionals of all kinds.

In our third meeting, she was more relaxed, more trusting, and even able to joke and smile on occasion. She talked about her own youth in Louisiana and eventually told me that she plans to begin working soon as a community health worker.

Her distrust of school personnel did not lessen. She believes that California teachers are more prejudiced toward blacks, less motivated to teach, more prone to keep students behind and less concerned about students. She told me that she had already requested a transfer for Paul. On several occasions, she has abruptly switched schools for his older brothers.

The mother became more cooperative as the interviews progressed. This came about as she realized that I was independent of the school system, really concerned about her child, and willing to listen and observe rather than to criticize and blame. She responded positively to my handling of the school consultation since she saw me as a professional assistant to her. I point out this change in our relationship in an effort to balance my initial view of her as a defensive, rigid, hostile, suspicious woman. This change was most noticeable when she spoke about her own life.

She told me that she has three older sisters and one brother. She grew up on a farm in Louisiana and enjoyed many aspects of the quiet, country life. One traumatic event which she mentioned twice was an unexpected, sudden illness in her father when she was six that left him blind. She and her siblings were expected to work on the farm and, at a young age, she learned to sew, iron and cook. "My mother expected us to look after ourselves."

I did not learn much about the quality of her marriage. She told me that she and her husband separated when Paul was three, but maintained contact in Indiana as well as in California. She feels Paul is similar to his father because both are quiet, have few friends, and seem to prefer being by themselves.

Interviews with Paul

First Interview. There was some confusion around the first interview because Mrs. Dumont misunderstood my request for an initial meeting with her. Rather than coming to see me alone, she, instead, brought Paul and so I saw her for the first 25 minutes and Paul for the last 25.

He appeared withdrawn, shy, inhibited and fearful at our initial contact in the hallway. He immediately sat down, uneasily scanned the office and awaited more words from me. After I introduced myself and let him know about our future meetings, the games and toys in the office, and that I wanted to get acquainted, we began to talk. Initially, he was quiet and reluctant to explore the toy cabinet. Replies to various general questions about school, home and his activities were brief and unenthusiastic until I asked him about sports. He was eager to talk about baseball and basketball and for the remainder of the hour he cheerfully told me about his play at a local recreation center. We later talked about the loss of Mr. Arthur, his former teacher, his interest in animals, and, finally, his feelings regarding the move from Indiana to California.

Much of the first hour can be understood as his desire to communicate his feelings about the absence of a constant father figure in his life. When we talked about baseball, he wanted to tell me about the coach. His idealization of the coach was apparent. When we talked about school, he spent several minutes telling me about his previous teacher, Mr. Arthur. When I became curious about the difference between Mr. Arthur and Miss Lane, he told me that Mr. Arthur took the students on field trips, sometimes played basketball with them, and understood the students better. Miss Lane, on the other hand, did not want to take the children on trips and knew little about sports.

He ended the hour by telling me about his pets here and in Indiana. There were many references to animals biting people. His dog, Dynamite, tries to bite him on the leg but doesn't hurt him. After telling me that he had to leave one of his dogs with his aunt in Indiana, he recalled that this dog would wake his father up by biting his toes and protected the house because "he would bite anyone trying to come in." Part of the reason the dog was given to his aunt was to "prevent people from stealing" from her farm.

We ended the interview after he told me that he liked Indiana better than California because it snowed and rained there and he had more animals.

Second Interview. Paul felt more comfortable in exploring the office this hour and, at times, was intrigued with some of the toys. Early in the hour, he picked up the dart gun and quickly shot it at a bull's-eye on the wall, then, dropped it immediately and did not play with it again. Instead, we played checkers for most of the hour.

During our game, we talked about school, his father and Maxwell, a 17-year-old boy who has recently joined the household and shares a room with Paul. He said that he does things with his father like going to wrestling matches and baseball games. He volunteered that his father is not home when he goes to bed because he works at night. This sounded like his explanation for the separation. Later in the hour, he told me that Maxwell joined the family last year because his father sent him away.

Paul played a checker game using unusual rules and ambiguous strategies. Often, he would ignore an obvious move. He changed rules frequently but not in the service of winning the game. During the game, he became absorbed in an adjoining chess set. He tried to place the small pawns within the larger kings, queens and bishops. Then he stacked the various chess players in order to build a tower. He also was briefly intrigued with the nesting barrels, hiding the small barrels in the larger one.

Toward the end of the hour, he noticed some toy cars and illustrated how he could tow four of them using a truck. His desire to connect toys to each other was prominent in this hour as well as in later hours.

Third Interview. This was the most difficult one of the four because Paul was very quiet, withdrawn, and unwilling to either play or talk. He spent several minutes playing with his hands or curling his hair with his fingers. A few times, he turned away from me and stared silently at a poster on the wall.

In the last 10 minutes, he talked a great deal about a recent painful experience at a baseball game. He and four of his friends were replaced by older boys by the coach and team captain. He was surprised and immediately quit the team and vowed not to play baseball again this year, even though he was invited by the other four friends to join their new team. He said that his friends were angry, too, and wanted to kill the coach.

At the very end of the hour he talked about his relationship with his brothers. He said that they tease each other and he reacts by throwing books at them and then running away and hiding.

Fourth Interview. Paul felt more at ease in sharing fantasies with me than during the third session. He explored the toy cabinets and examined many things slowly and with a serious intent. He found the doctor kit and enjoyed examining the syringes and stethoscope. He used the stethoscope to listen to his heart, and then kept it around his neck for most of the hour.

After finding several cars and connecting them in a long line, he noticed the play animals and wanted to tell me their names and a short story about them. He identified several—a bear, moose, camel, dinosaur, crocodile, etc.—and as he talked, he placed them on the top of the cabinet. Then he told me that if one should fall off, it would die because the crocodiles in the drawer would eat them. Finally, he noticed the dart gun and at close range took several shots at the animals and play cars. After a few shots, he left the animals and looked at other things.

A few times he mentioned that his nephew, Maurice, destroys some of his, Paul's, toy planes and cars.

After noticing a toy rabbit, he told me he wanted to shoot one at the park and inquired whether I had ever eaten one. At around the same time, he noticed the play soldiers and slowly identified their weapons for me—i.e., rifles, bazookas, grenades and machine guns.

His play with the frog and fox puppets was most revealing. He had the fantasy of using the frog puppet to scare Maurice. When I asked how, he said he would put it on a stick, go into his nephew's room and say "bogey, bogey." He then placed a fox puppet with a snarling mouth on one hand and a dog on his other and proceeded to show me their fight. The fox is going to eat the dog, but the dog puts the fox's foot in his mouth, then the dog grabs the stomach and finally bites the fox's tongue. He decides that the fox dies when his tongue is bitten.

He left this play quickly and invited me to play pick-up sticks. He won a few games and I won one. I noticed that he tried to scare me as I moved. I commented that he wanted to scare Maurice as well, and I inquired whether he ever was scared by anything. He quickly said, "sure," and told me that he was scared the night before. He said that there was a full moon and, hence, the werewolf came out. He said that the werewolf kills people at night but doesn't hurt anyone in the morning.

As we parted, I was aware of his confusion about whether to express his feelings about not seeing me anymore.

School Consultation

In the meeting with the teacher, principal, school social worker and psychologist, it was learned that Paul rarely plays with others, even when invited, seems totally apathetic and difficult to engage, barks like a dog when angry and pretends to be other people. The psychologist reported that Paul spent a long time pretending to be a boy named Frank, who the psychologist had deduced was an actual old friend from Indiana.

They are fairly sure that Paul killed the class' pet salamander. His difficulty in controlling himself has led to a reduced school schedule, even in this very small, special class. The staff is concerned about Paul's capacity to transfer to junior high school next year. I agreed to convey our recommendations to the school, when our evaluation was more complete.

Psychological Testing (Summary)

The psychologist was impressed with Paul's immaturity. He is confused at some very basic levels. His conception of human beings is very disturbed in that he rarely connects human feelings with external events. He was very preoccupied with aggression and almost every story he told was filled with uninhibited, sadistic content. Punishments were meted out for minor fantasy infractions and generally they involved years of imprisonment and death. He continued to express sadistic fantasies in his stories of animals as he did in the clinical interviews.

His drawings of a girl and a boy pointed to the minimal differentiation he makes between the sexes.

In his performance tasks, he showed more skill at mechanical than verbal tests. His memory was poor and there was considerable confusion evident in his perceptual capacity. There was a marked inability to concentrate and some question about whether he was hallucinating. His inability to make obvious causal connections was very pronounced, as was his concrete thinking.

The testing data were consistent with either a severe borderline state with numerous ego deficits or an incipient pre-adolescent psychosis.

Dynamic Formulation

Paul shows multiple areas of severe ego deficits. These include major difficulty in cognition and learning, impulse control and interpersonal relationships. Central to the dynamics are primitive-sadistic aggressive fantasies and impulses which are managed poorly by equally primitive defenses (isolation and/or bizarre behavior). While his relationships are meager and unsatisfying, he longs for connections to idealized figures who either disappear or are insufficiently present. The family support system does not provide the help he requires.

Despite the severity and pervasiveness of his problems, Paul was able to make contact with me, thus suggesting his capacity to use a therapeutic relationship.

Recommendation

The psychologist and I agree that outpatient psychotherapy would be insufficient in helping Paul with his many problems. We feel that his placement in a residential center would be the most reasonable alternative in view of the extensive psychopathology. In such a setting, the highly structured milieu may be able to promote his educational development, relieve some of his fear and anxiety, and foster the growth of various ego capacities not yet realized. This therapeutic environment should also include intensive, direct psychotherapy. His placement would also remove him from an environmental setting which presently offers little support and may, unintentionally, contribute to his pathology. I will discuss this recommendation with Mrs. Dumont and, if she decides it would be best, I will help her contact the necessary people in the Department of Social Services.

First Interpretive Interview

I met with Mrs. Dumont and told her that I had met with the school, the psychologist, and a senior staff member to assess Paul's difficulties and decide what would be most helpful.

Earlier in our meetings, I had told Mrs. Dumont that Paul was worried, depressed, concerned with loss, and I now elaborated on how his difficulties interfere with his ability to learn in school. In this meeting, I stressed that I was worried about him now and about his future. I also told her that Paul keeps his feelings to himself but that in our meetings I could tell that he is preoccupied with people hurting one another. I told her that I worried about him getting into trouble in his adolescence by hurting himself or someone else. I said that his relative withdrawal from other children is, in many ways, an attempt to lessen many of his anxieties and fears and is not done merely because he likes to be alone. Although I could not be exact about the nature of his fears, I did say that it is helpful when children verbalize their worries and for Paul to do this, it would take a long-term therapeutic relationship with someone he could trust.

I told her that Paul needed more than outpatient therapy; I said he needed to live in a home where trained professionals could help him on a 24-hour basis. I pointed out that he was young and that it was a good time to help him since in five to ten years, changes would be much more difficult. We discussed his need to learn skills like math, spelling, reading and writing in order to find a satisfying job some day and that, as long as he was absorbed in his worries, he could not concentrate on school tasks. I cited the known experience of child therapists that children usually do better in school after they have come to understand their fears. I agreed with her that less than three hours of schooling daily, which he is now obtaining, were insufficient for Paul's growth.

After I finished with much of my brief assessment, I asked for her thoughts and was surprised by her reaction. I expected her to be very resistant but instead she told me that she had been wondering why Paul didn't play much with other children. She said that doctors had told her in the past not to worry about him—that he would grow out of it. I was the first doctor who said he was worried about her son. It was clear that she appreciated my desire to see Paul develop into a happier, more competent, less anxious man. She did not get upset. She, almost blandly, said that I have more training than she has and that she wants to do what is best for him. Then she asked a series of questions about what I recommended. Are those places like this around? What are they like? Is there a guarantee that it would help? Would he visit the family? How do they live? How would she pay for it?

I told her that they were not hospitals with locked rooms. They were more like schools. I explained the procedure she would follow if she agreed with my recommendation. I told her that we would talk more about this, that she would undoubtedly have more questions, and that I understood the decision had implications for the whole family.

She told me she would discuss it with Paul. I predicted he would find the thought of being separated from his family for a while very upsetting. I predicted he would say that he did not want to go, but I pointed out to her that his perspective is different from ours. We are concerned with his future—his future family, his job, his education—while he would naturally be more concerned about his current life.

We ended the meeting on a cordial note and agreed to meet again.

In our next session, Mrs. Dumont continued to accept the recommendation and discussed with me Paul's naturally worried response and the reactions of her family. I was impressed with the way she was handling the situation and conveyed this to her. She had other questions, which I answered as fully as I could, and together we arranged for her meetings with the placement worker.

Discussion

As one can see from the case report, Paul is a severely disturbed boy. There are indications from the history, the clinical interviews, the psychological testing and the school report that Paul's functioning is severely and chronically impaired. He does not learn at school; even his special class cannot maintain him for a full school day. He has few friends and even fewer at school. His social skills are limited. Basic functions such as speech are impaired—he often mumbles or is inaudible. He experiences his world as precarious, unsafe and unpredictable. Often, he appears confused and confusing to others. He has serious difficulty in modulating his affective responses to external or internal stimuli. Expressions of aggression and efforts to control these preoccupy him and he manages them in a primitive way. Either he withdraws and hides from others or he behaves in strange ways— like an angry, barking dog. Neither effort at relieving his fears and anxiety helps him greatly. On the contrary, these reactions deepen his isolation and estrangement from others. This further confuses and frightens Paul and heightens his sense that the world is unjust and depriving.

There are few supports in his home. His yearned-for father is away, despite regular contact. Paul cannot make sense of this. His mother, who vigorously maintains that all is well with Paul, leaves him once again to fend for himself with few resources. It is remarkable that Paul speaks so little of his brothers and sister, suggesting that he does not see them as helpful. When he speaks of others, they are idealized, no longer available or depriving.

His play and his fantasy suggest intense conflict with primitive and sadistic impulses. This is most clearly illustrated in the account of the puppet play with the fox and the dog in which biting, destroying and dying are portrayed. We never learn what causes the fight; cognitive content remains unclear. We can infer from this that whatever propelled the fantasies, these become so overwhelming that Paul cannot stop to convey their meaning. Probably he has so little distance from such terrifying thoughts that he makes little rational sense of them himself. Instead, confusion seems to color much of his thinking. Inner and outer boundaries seem unclear, which is understandable given that his external world is not now, nor has it ever been, sufficiently safe and protecting.

We can see how the evaluator is led to his recommendation for a therapeutic environment for Paul, rather than a recommendation for outpatient treatment alone. The combination of the severity and pervasiveness of Paul's disturbance and the insufficient environmental supports in his home and school led to the correct recommendation to place this child in a residential treatment center. Such a setting ought ideally to combine:

1) a structured, reliable and consistent day-to-day pattern of living;

2) a therapeutic milieu which can attune itself to Paul's need to develop reality testing, impulse control, clearer boundaries between his thoughts and actions, and between self and others, as well as the development of social and educational skills; and

3) intensive, individual psychotherapy.

Although the evaluator was concerned that Paul's mother would resist the recommendations, she did not. He correctly remained available to help her make the necessary arrangements for such placement, encouraging her to explore her questions, reservations and concerns. We consider this evaluation to be a thorough and careful one. In particular, the post-diagnostic sessions with the mother are well and sensitively handled.

CASE 4—MARIA RAMIREZ

Identifying Data

Maria is 14, the middle child in a family of three girls. She is presently in the ninth grade at a public junior high school, where she does very well. She lives at home with her mother and her younger sister, Nina, age 12. Her older sister, Carmen, is 19 and has been out of the home for several years.

Referral

Maria's mother originally applied for help for Nina, who had run away from home for several days. Nine has begun treatment and now the mother reports that she is also upset with Maria's defiance, and fears that both girls will become involved with boys, hinting at worries about their becoming pregnant. The mother is also concerned about Maria's envy and jealousy of Nina and the constant fighting between the two sisters. Mrs. Ramirez seems to favor Nina and, at present, is angrier at Maria. She complains about the girl's unresponsiveness, secretiveness and greater loyalty to the father, who has been out of the home since Maria was seven. Mrs. Ramirez is bitter about the father's failure to help support the family, his disinterest in them, and the burden this placed upon her in raising her three girls. Mr.

Ramirez has remarried and has visited the family only three or four times since his absence. The mother's rage with Maria was precipitated by a letter recently written by the father to Maria, which Mrs. Ramirez brought with her to the first interview as "evidence" of Maria's greater loyalty to the father than to her her. The mother seemed to demonstrate no guilt about intercepting and opening her daughter's mail and, in general, appeared unsympathetic toward Maria.

The impression of Mrs. Ramirez, gained during Nina's evaluation, was of a burdened, disturbed, working-class woman who felt considerable anger toward all her children. She, herself, had had a stormy adolescence and, in fact, became pregnant before she married Mr. Ramirez. Her complaints and anger were so great during Maria's evaluation that it was impossible to gather any developmental history. Considering this and the information already available from Nina's evaluation and Maria's age and developmental stage, I decided to see Maria next.

Intake with Maria

Maria is a tall, precociously mature, physically beautiful 14-year-old. She seated herself as far away from me as possible, hung her head almost continuously throughout the hour, and wept silently and copiously as she described her situation. She doubts that her mother can change. She spent most of the hour describing how mother treats her and Carmen, her oldest sister, with whom she feels a strong kinship. Nina clearly seems the "favorite" of the three. Mother continually allies herself with Nina and becomes wrathful when the other girls even "bitch" at Nina. Maria encounters continual accusations that she would end up "no good" (this hinted at in sexual terms), coupled with her mother's refusal to allow her to live elsewhere. Maria believes that her mother links her to her father (this is a relatively astute observation); she also believes that Nina had a different father, although they share the same surname. "Nina doesn't even look like him," she said, to confirm her belief in different parentage. Her conversation was a composite of two viewpoints: 1) Father is great; he may be my ticket out of an intolerable situation;

2) the more realistic observation that she hasn't seen her father in years and—although he writes lovingly—he hasn't done much to help.

Near the end of the hour, she looked at me and spoke more directly. Nevertheless, she declined my offer of help—even after we cleared away the idea that "only nuts come to shrinks." I felt that her resistance was connected to the concern that coming into treatment would mean that something was wrong with *her*, not with her mother. This viewpoint was by no means entirely defensive, inappropriate or maladaptive. Furthermore, entering treatment would appear as a submission and capitulation to mother's wishes and attitudes toward Maria.

The most noticeable change in her affect occurred when Maria, visibly brightening, recounted her work the previous summer in a nursery school. At the time, she lived with her sister, Carmen. Speaking lovingly of the children at school, she discussed her ambition to become a teacher.

Her ambivalence about further help was intense and almost palpable. Holding me beyond the end of the hour, Maria became more expressive in announcing that her mother will insist on extracting from her what she has stated to me in confidence. She has seen her mother do this with Nina when she has returned from therapy sessions. This would surely precipitate further "hassles" with mother—a prospect which seems, at the least, uninviting. I discussed with Maria what I'd tell her mother about our talk. I acknowledged her wish not to enter treatment, and we talked of some of the bases for her decision. At the end of the session, I placed my professional card on the table (she had to reach to pick it up) so that, *if she chose*, she could use it in the future; she took it with her.

Formulation and Disposition

Maria appears to be a moderately depressed, precocious, appealing adolescent. She has adjusted to a nearly intolerable family situation by keeping to herself, developing a relatively realistic appraisal of her mother's pathology, constricting her expression and activity somewhat, using her older sister as a separate source of identification and emotional succor, and overidealizing her absent father. At the same time, she is able to relate interpersonally and performs well in school. In addition, she appears to have no impairment in reality sense or judgment, continues to maintain aspiration for achievement and independence, and, despite her mother's fears, has not indulged in acting-out or self-destructive behavior. In sum, Maria is an enormously appealing adolescent who, upon more detailed examination, may show scars of greater deprivation but who now presents an intact ego, with depressive features. My comfort in respecting Maria's choice to decline (or defer) therapy at this point results from my appraisal that she is, in the face of difficult familial circumstances, functioning well, and that entering treatment at her mother's behest would risk the necessary distance which she has rightfully established from her mother. Taken together, these seem highly appropriate adolescent efforts.

Recommendation

Further treatment is not recommended unless and until such time that Maria chooses to seek it on her own initiative.

Post-Diagnostic Interview

I met with Mrs. Ramirez subsequent to my interview with Maria. I told her that, while I thoroughly appreciated the difficulties she faced in raising her daughters and understood fully her wish to be more appreciated than a father who had given so little to his children, our experience indicated Maria's behavior was, in many ways, typical of teenagers and, outside of the family, I thought that Maria was doing very well. I let her know that insisting that Maria begin treatment now would probably be unproductive and wasteful of her money and effort. The mother grudgingly accepted this recommendation.

Discussion

It is unlikely that Maria would have entered treatment, in any productive sense, no matter what the therapist recommended. However, in this instance, one sees a girl whose rebelliousness towards her mother helps her progress towards independence and defends her against an attachment and an identification with a woman whose reality testing is inadequate and whose subtle messages of inevitable wrongdoing exert pressures to keep the girl within the family orbit. The evaluator is faced with a difficult decision. Maria is depressed, struggling too precociously to achieve independence and clearly overidealizing a father who can give her little. In theory, these are adolescent difficulties which could be helped by therapy. However, given the context of the referral and the mother's enormous intrusiveness, which Maria must ward off massively, a recommendation for therapy carries the risk of promoting regression and breaking into defenses which are necessary and adaptive. We agree with the therapist's choice to honor Maria's autonomy and resistance to treatment, despite clear evidence of Maria's own intense ambivalence.

Several technical features of this evaluation are worth noting. Maria and her mother were seen by someone other than Nina's therapist. The referral of a second family member when one is already in treatment always poses the tricky question of who shall do the assessment. In this case, the intense sibling rivalry clearly dictated that a different therapist was needed. The potential problem of an intense loyalty conflict outweighs the advantage of the prior knowledge and familiarity which Nina's therapist already has.

A second issue relates to the rapidity with which the adolescent is seen here. The gathering of developmental information is deferred in favor of a more rapid connection and contact with a youngster who, by age and stage, must take greater responsibility for the therapeutic work. The need to appreciate the efforts made by adolescents to move away from the primary family dictates that the most careful consideration be given to the timing and sequencing of the diagnostic interview series.

*   *   *

An overview of the four cases we have presented demonstrates a number of distinctions. The children and their families are different in ages, developmental phases, socioeconomic and educational levels, family circumstances, severity of disturbances, and accessibility to help. A careful reading of each evaluation also reveals the differences in therapeutic style, despite a common frame of theoretical reference. However, beyond these differences, each of these cases leads to a different set of recommendations. In Mark's case, direct outpatient psychotherapy was unnecessary, though considerable therapeutic benefit is achieved by attention to valuable environmental changes and some therapeutic help to his parents. Alicia presents the combination of pathology which requires direct intervention in a family support system which makes outpatient psychotherapy feasible. By contrast, Paul's disturbance is so severe and the environmental support system so insufficient, that outpatient treatment alone would be inadequate. A more total program is required if we are to try to help repair the already extensive damage and to promote growth.

Finally, Maria's case illustrates the need to temper therapeutic zeal with common sense, which recognizes the limitations of therapy. Maria's motivation is not just lacking; she, herself, is all too painfully aware that the risk of entering therapy is greater than the appeal it holds for her. She knows this far better than we can and was fortunate to have an evaluator who could hear and respect this knowledge.

FURTHER READING

Bornstein, Berta (1935), Analysis of a Phobia in a Two-and-One-Half-Year-Old Child. *Psychoanalytic Quarterly*, 4:93-119.
Ekstein, Rudolf and Wallerstein, Judith (1956), Observations on Psychotherapy of Borderline and Psychotic Children. *Psychoanalytic Study of the Child*, 11:303-311.
Fraiberg, Selma (1955), Some Considerations in the Introduction to Therapy in Puberty. *Psychoanalytic Study of the Child*, 10:264-286.
Freud, Anna (1962), Assessment of Childhood Disturbances. *Psychoanalytic Study of the Child*, 17:149-158.
Friedman, Seymour W. (1966), The Diagnostic Process as Part of the Treatment Process. *Reiss-Davis Clinic Bulletin*, 3:62-67.
Huber, Jack T. (1968), *Report Writing in Psychology and Psychiatry*. New York: Harper and Row.
Korner, Analiese and Opsvig, Paul (1966), Developmental Considerations in Diagnosis and Treatment—A Case Illustration. *Journal of the American Academy of Child Psychiatry*, 5:594-616.
Meers, Dale R. (1970), Contributions of a Ghetto Culture to Symptom Formation. *Psychoanalytic Study of the Child*, 25:209-230.
Strunk, William Jr. and White, E. B. (1972), *The Elements of Style*. New York: The Macmillan Company.
Wenar, C. (1963), The Reliability of Developmental Histories. *Psychosomatic Medicine*, 25:505-509.

8

The Role of

Psychological Testing

In two of the four diagnostic evaluations in the last chapter, psychological testing was sought by the evaluator as part of the initial assessment. While psychological testing is not necessary for all children, it can be of great diagnostic help when carefully and properly integrated as part of a complete assessment.

All too often, psychological tests have been surrounded by an aura of magic. Tests are seen as some sort of divining rod which mysteriously taps levels of personality not available to the less penetrating eye of the clinician. Results are perceived as absolute views into the interior structure of the psyche almost as if they, the tests, were the x-rays of the mind. This view has led to a vast overmystification of the tests and their capacities. Tests are, in fact, only stan-

dardized clinical instruments. The real subject matter of the tests is behavior and the real tool of the tester is clinical inference. Consequently, test results are not primarily a function of tests themselves as instruments but depend on the skill of the test interpreter, just as the results of the clinical interview depend upon the inferential skills of the therapist. Viewed this way, tests can add immeasurably to our understanding, but they, too, are subject to error and imprecision. They may add to our information and round out the clinical picture but cannot replace the clinical assessment.

In contrast to the clinical interview, the field of observation during testing is markedly reduced by the presence of standardized stimuli. This makes it possible to record the moment-to-moment behavior in a way that is qualitatively different from that which the clinical interview permits. Such detailed records can then be compared to standardized responses. Furthermore, the demand for interaction which the testing situation places upon the clinician is minimal in contrast to the interview situation, thus freeing energy for observational purposes. Further still, projective tests, in particular, pull for responses that may reflect levels of conflict of which the patient is unaware and which may not be as readily seen in the clinical interview. This "pull" is inherent in the nature of the stimuli (for example, ink-blots). Tests of intellectual function also provide information which is not as readily available in the clinical interview. In addition to their capacity to provide a more precise, general estimate of the multiple components of intellectual capacities, they can shed light upon cognitive style, developmental processes, and the degree to which thinking is free of contamination by intrusive affects or impulses. These tests, therefore, help us to better understand the individual's reality-orientation and quality of thinking.

Tests can be useful in clarifying the depth and pervasiveness of pathology, the nature of specific conflicts, the nature, quality and impairments of cognitive functions, the nature of affects, the existence of primitive processes and the nature and effectiveness of ego strengths and defenses. Also, important differential diagnostic questions may sometimes be illuminated more precisely. For example, subtle signs of organic impairment or incipient psychotic processes may be elicited by careful psychological tests.

In recent years, psychological tests have fallen into some disrepute. Tests have been attacked as culturally biased and favoring those with verbal skills. They have also been criticized when used to pigeonhole and label people. Such criticisms have validity; nevertheless, when used carefully and with proper respect for the cultural background and individual uniqueness of people, tests remain a valuable adjunct to the clinical work.

When and how to refer for psychological tests are important considerations. We have already indicated that all evaluations do not require a battery of psychological tests. Our psychologist colleagues appropriately complain about ambiguous, ill-defined and inappropriate test referrals. The most useful results typically are achieved when the clinician phrases his questions and the areas of his concern as precisely as possible. This not only is useful to the psychologist, but serves to clarify the questions which confuse the clinician, pointing toward those matters which require further understanding. For example, test referrals which request differentiation between several specific diagnostic possibilities or address particular questions about the primitivity of observed defenses are infinitely better than test referrals which ask only "Please do an I.Q. and a Rorschach."

Children and their parents should be prepared for tests simply and forthrightly. If possible a direct personal introduction to the tester is extremely valuable. The child should know that you will expect to see him during the testing and after the tests are complete. Without this preparation, many children experience the referral as an abandonment.

Parental permission should be obtained before testing and parents should be informed of your reasons for a testing referral. Similarly, they should be assured that the tests results will be discussed with them, as part of your total impressions and recommendations. Whenever possible, we think that the clinician responsible for the overall assessment, rather than the tester, should convey a summary of the test findings to the family. If there are separate fees for the testing, this, of course, should be discussed in advance.

Finally, it must be kept in mind that the written report of the psychological testing is written for the referring clinician and the official records. Like any other part of the "case file," it is confidential and not automatically available to parents, school physicians, probation officers, etc. However, where a written report may help the parents, the school, the physician or some other caretaker to understand better, it is possible to provide, selectively, a brief and clear written summary of the major explanatory findings. By and large, such written summaries, as well as verbal accounts, are best couched in non-technical language. In particular, precise I.Q. scores are often misunderstood and misused and, therefore, should be conveyed only with the greatest caution and judgment.

FURTHER READING

Heiman, Nanette and Cooper, Shirley (1959), An Experiment in Clinical Integration. *Journal of the Hillside Hospital.*
Korner, Analiese (1962), Developmental Diagnostic Dimensions as Seen Through Psychological Tests. *Journal of Projective Techniques.* 26:201-211.
Lourie, Reginald S. and Rieger, Rebecca E. (1974), Psychiatric and Psychological Examination of Children. In: *American Handbook of Psychiatry*, Vol. II, New York: Basic Books.

9

Other Aids to
Diagnostic Assessment

SPECIAL EDUCATIONAL ASSESSMENT

Usually, the children referred to us are in school. Frequently, some difficulties in learning and school adjustment are part of their problems. The relationship between psychological difficulties and learning problems has been well documented. For many youngsters, emotional problems are manifested by an inability to learn or to learn as fully as their intellectual capacity would otherwise permit.

The shame and humiliation which youngsters experience when they are unable to keep up with their peers create for them a sense of incompetence, a vulnerability to failure and a reduced motivation or ability to try or to risk. Learning requires some assertive reaching out to understand. When failure to learn occurs, it may impair or constrict the ability to reach toward knowledge and knowing. For some, heightened motoric activity becomes the only avenue for redeeming self-esteem, with the concomitant result that such youngsters fail even further to "take in" knowledge.

Experience with the treatment of children suggests that those unable to learn because of emotional difficulties may become so withdrawn or so hyperactive that the learning disorder deepens. For others, the learning problems are at the root of the emotional disorder.

Whatever the etiology, the relationship between emotional difficulties and learning is a highly correlated one.

For some children, psychological assessment is not complete without fuller clarification of their precise educational difficulties. Similarly, a psychological treatment plan may be insufficient to alleviate learning problems. Such youngsters additionally need educational diagnosis and planning. This form of early detection, diagnosis, and educational planning can be central in the prevention of the entrenchment of problems which preclude learning and normal social and emotional development.

There is a growing group of trained and experienced individuals in the field of special education, who can diagnose, prescribe educationally, and consult with therapists to enhance the therapists' understanding of the learning process and broaden the perspective within which therapists treat children.

When such a specialist is available, an educational assessment, in selected cases, can be an invaluable adjunct to the diagnostic and treatment planning process. Such an educational assessment generally involves three stages:

1) A review of the child's school record, including achievement levels, prior testing, teacher evaluations and reports from school counselors, social workers and psychologists.

2) Classroom observations directed toward an understanding of the child's functioning, academically and socially, as well as a knowledge of the classroom environment. This environment must be understood in order to later provide classroom recommendations which are relevant and realistic and which will enhance learning and socialization. The special education teacher's firsthand knowledge of and experiences with classroom teaching provide an essential bridge between therapeutic personnel and the classroom teacher.

3) A formal evaluation of the child's current academic performance, intellectual potential, learning style and learning impairments. This includes assessment of perceptual, cognitive and motor skills. Tests used include instruments to help tap the child's receptive and expressive language skills, phonic skills, reading comprehension, math skills, conceptual development, visual and auditory perceptual skills, and gross and fine motor skills.

As with other testing procedures, the educational specialist and the therapist must be aware that some tests currently in use are "culture-bound" and must therefore be reviewed with a sensitive understanding of the value and importance of different sociocultural life experiences. Test results must be viewed along with other information in arriving at a comprehensive picture of the child's emotional and educational difficulties and assets. They may lead to specific recommendations which can include tutoring, classroom strategies, consultation with classroom teachers, assignment to special classes or schools, work with parents and small group learning sessions.

As described in the preceding section on psychological testing, thoughtfulness and care must be used in making the referral for an educational assessment and in the transmittal of the findings back to all the people concerned.

DIAGNOSTIC PLAY GROUPS

In recent years, a number of child treatment centers have developed play activity group programs for emotionally disturbed children. Generally, these groups have served as a primary modality of therapeutic work or as an adjunct to the individual treatment of the child and his family. These programs are not group therapy in the traditional sense. Verbal interaction and interpretation are not their principal stock-in-trade. Rather, these groups emphasize age- and phase-appropriate activities aimed at enhancing skill development, socialization with peers, and ability to pursue a task from its beginning to its completion, and opportunities for tension discharge through structured activity. They also provide the opportunity for brief exploration of behavior as it unfolds in the immediate "live" interaction.

Such groups help children who are loners, scapegoats, or fighters, and those who are shunned by peers. These children miss out on the growth and pleasure associated with normal group life. In addition to the therapeutic benefit offered by such groups, they can add, to the diagnostic assessment, important insights about the child and his style of interacting with peers and adults. During the diagnostic process, the placement of a child in a limited number of play group sessions can provide information about the child's behavior, skills, and peer relationships which are difficult to tap in the one-to-one diagnostic interview.

OTHER DIAGNOSTIC AIDS

Naturally, a complete diagnosis will include medical information from the child's pediatrician or family physician and a school report. While these are typically considered important sources of information, no data should be routinely sought without considering the implications involved in "seeking" the material or without prior discussion with the family. On occasion, more specialized information, such as a neurological or speech and hearing workup, will be useful.

In summary, the diagnostic evaluation of a child and his family may involve many procedures and many sources of information. However, we once again remind the beginner that "the most—with the least" is usually more beneficial than an interminably protracted process.

FURTHER READING

Long, N. G., Morse, W. C. and Newman, R. G. (1971), *Conflict in the Classroom.* Belmont, California: Wadsworth.

Newman, Ruth G. (1967), *Psychological Consultation in the Schools.* New York: Basic Books.

Redl, Fritz (1966), *When We Deal with Children.* New York: The Free Press.

Rieger, Rebecca, Schroeder, W. and Uschold, C. (1968), *Special Education: Children with Learning Problems.* New York: Oxford University Press.

Wineman, David (1959), The Life Space Interview. *Journal of Social Work,* 4:3-17.

10

Beginning Again

The diagnostic process with the new patient is only one form of "beginning." Typically, there are many disruptions in the course of a treatment which require beginning once again. The most common experiences which new therapists encounter are: 1) the transferred case—beginning with a patient who has had a prior therapist; and 2) those hours immediately following a vacation—beginning again after an interruption.

The following illustrations of these common situations are presented to clarify the technical and theoretical issues inherent in such events. The first two illustrations are reports of new therapists who have just begun the post-transfer work.

TRANSFERRED CASES

Case 1—Janice

This is the first post-transfer hour with Janice, a 12-year-old only child, who has been in treatment for 18 months. She was initially referred for "not minding," talking constantly in class and fighting at home and at school. She has difficulty learning. During the past 18 months, she saw a young woman therapist, who has completed her training and left the area. Janice made considerable gains in her past treatment, but the therapist felt there was more work to be done and Janice and her family agreed. The new therapist is also a young woman.

Janice's parents are described as severely impaired, with many somatic problems. Both are unemployed, the father as a result of a recent heart attack and subsequent psychotic episode. The new therapist's account follows:

I had met Janice and her parents briefly two days before this initial appointment, when they dropped by to schedule this meeting (they have no phone). Janice is pretty, but, like her mother, obese. She greeted me in that initial encounter with a shy smile, but said nothing.

For the first "official" appointment, I find Janice in the waiting room with her mother. They have arrived early, and I agree to see her 15 minutes before the scheduled starting time. In the waiting room, I say "Hi," and Janice says quickly, "I didn't recognize you for sure. I'm going to get my ears pierced tomorrow. Me and my friend, Betty." We walk together toward my office. Still in the hallway, I say, "Do you have the earrings picked out?" She replies, "I have some already. I picked out the silver ones; Betty picked out the gold ones. I can't wear big ones at school, because if someone fights with me, they might pull on them—so I'll only wear little ones in school."

This, and her subsequent remarks, are non-stop, and said with considerable nervousness. We reach the office; she sits down quickly and continues without looking around. Periodically, during her monologue, she observes, "I talk too much"—but goes right on. I listen.

At length, she discourses on the following topics: fighting at school; starting junior high in September where there "is lots of fighting"; she fights with kids on the block; "but Betty and I don't fight anymore"; Betty has a dog and Janice loves dogs and all animals. She wants to go to college to study astrology because she loves stars. She saw a program about animals and was interested in how they protect themselves. There was a snake that would lie on its back and play dead, when in danger. Sometimes she wishes she was an orphan in an orphanage, but big kids don't get adopted. Only the little

kids, "but they don't understand and don't even need all that attention, the way big kids do." She likes puppies and kittens and even
sharks. She saw the movie, "Jaws," and wonders if they used a real
man. It was scary when the shark bit off the man's leg: "How could
they use a real man for that? But it was too real, they must have.
Did you see it?"

I said that I didn't see it, but that I was sure they didn't use a real
man. I said that the shark wasn't real either, but I acknowledged that
it must have been pretty scary.

Janice responds, "It looked real, with blood and everything."

She now looks at the plant on my desk and says, "I like plants—
except mine die. I had one that I really liked. I watered it and kept
it in the light, but that didn't help. I wished I could kill it, before it
died. No!" (Nervous giggle.)

She talks next about her wish that she could be thin, before starting junior high. "I like to wear pants to cover myself. One girl wears
dresses to school—real short, so she looks like . . . a whore—pardon
my language." She talks about having few clothes because her parents
are poor. They weren't always poor when her father worked. She
recalls that her grandfather used to buy her many things. She was
his favorite; he liked her better than all of his grandchildren, and
he even liked her better than her mother. She liked that. Her father
isn't like that; he always sides with her mother. She fights with her
mother, "I shouldn't do that."

Nobody is really on her side, so she wants to save up money and
have things all to herself. If she had her own TV, she'd only let her
father watch it after she saw her programs. Now she has to watch
what her father wants. "I have to listen whether I want to or not.
It's funny, the doctor—you're my second—said my ears are fine,
but sometimes I don't hear what people say to me and I talk too
much."

I comment, "Maybe sometimes you don't hear, because it's the only
way you can be alone. Miss F. (previous therapist) told me that
you don't have a room of your own and it's hard sometimes to have
privacy. Miss F. told me some things about you; maybe you'll tell
me more."

Janice says, "O.K.," but looks sad.

Discussion

This rich, first transfer hour offers a "table of contents" for the ongoing treatment. Janice clearly portrays her many conflicts, continuing concerns, and some of the roots of these. One can see how the ongoing issues are woven together with some immediate and specific concerns about beginning again with her new therapist. A review of Janice's discourse points to the following important areas and their relationship to the new situation:

1) The early arrival and the initial nervousness, the uncertain recognition of her new therapist and her non-stop talk are clear evidence of her anxiety. One can view the endless talk as a defensive effort to master and control her discomfort about the new situation, though she also, typically, uses talk defensively to screen "what she can't hear." However, the talk is informative as well as defensive.

2) The content concerns itself with all the things that worry Janice, some of which are presented directly, while others are more tangentially suggested. Among her "topics" are:

a) beginning a new school, which we can be fairly sure also represents her concern about beginning with a new worker;

b) fighting and its various vicissitudes;

c) not having enough for herself and never feeling certain that she will ever have enough. Once again, while this issue is characteristic for Janice, its appearance here may well relate to the loss of the previous therapist;

d) obesity, and her conflicts about this: If only she could be thin for the new school; yet thin girls wear short skirts and may risk being thought of as "a whore";

e) the dangers in her world, her confusion about what dangers are real and how people and animals can protect themselves from these;

f) her notice of the therapist's plant—a first look at the new room—ushers in the thoughts about how hard it is to keep treasured things alive and well. It is likely that this theme relates to her ambivalent concern about her recently ill father, the loss of her grandfather, and the recent departure of her first therapist. Her active angry thought, "I wished I could kill it before it died," is followed quickly by a disclaimer;

g) being chosen and special appears in many guises—selecting special earrings, the wish to be a specially chosen orphan, and the account of her lost specialness in her relationship to her grandfather. We can also speculate about her fantasies of lost specialness to her former therapist and how she was "chosen" by the current one;

    h) her problems with attending, hearing and learning close the hour and include the only overt reference to her previous therapist.

The new therapist is apparently "clued-in" to many of these overt and subtle themes. She listens carefully, permitting the monologue to proceed. She does not intrude with her own agenda, although she is alert to the need to bridge from the old to the new.

This hour also illustrates well that interviews do not begin in the office; the work begins in the waiting room and the hallway. The new therapist properly chooses to begin where the patient is now, by expressing interest in Janice's comments about her earrings. Wittingly or not, she immediately puts the issue of "choosing" before Janice. From the account, the therapist chooses only two other moments in which to speak. The first reassures Janice about what dangers are real—which, nevertheless, may not offer much comfort. She follows this typical novice's impulse with a genuinely empathic remark about how scary such thoughts are. Her last comments center around a gentle interpretation—which is quite to the point—of Janice's selective hearing and how that might serve her. This content permits her to bring the old therapist into the discussion, conveying to Janice her continuity with Miss F., and opens the possibility for the new therapist to offer a tentative "contract" for continuing work.

Janice seems o accept the contract, but her sad demeanor alerts us to the need for further working through of the loss and the transition.

Case 2—Samuel

Samuel, 13, a seductive, attractive boy, was transferred from his first therapist, Dr. Farley, who had seen him for about two months. Dr. Farley felt that he had had little, if any, impact on the boy. The majority of their time was spent in playing chess, which the boy usually won, since he was one of the city school chess champions. Just as his first therapist was leaving, Sam's anxious mother made arrangements for him to be interviewed for placement with a Big Brother.

In his first two hours with me, the boy sat (although it was impossible for him to remain physically still) and talked throughout the hours—this, a complete reversal of his behavior with the first therapist. Much of this talk consisted in bravado—tales of being involved in somewhat dangerous, illegal, aggressive or sexual activities —whose implied theme was that we two worldly men could understand these things. Sam expressed much verbalized anger against his mother, father and siblings and against "queers" and authority figures. He spoke of a fantasy about possessing a magical sense of being protected: Nothing untoward would happen to him; he would always escape detection.

At the beginning of the third hour, Sam appeared in a complete outfit of new clothes. He told me how he had purchased them all by himself and was obviously asking for approval. Suddenly, he informed me that he had been thinking about not coming to the clinic during the summer. I commented that it was his decision whether or not to come and that I did not want him to come for any reason except his own desire to do so. Then I asked if we might discuss this decision. He replied that he wanted to think about it first—not talk.

Suddenly, he told me of a dream. He had gone to Big Brothers, where they lined up several men against the wall—"like in a police lineup"—and told him to choose a Big Brother. I asked if there were anyone familiar there. With a guarded look, Sam told me that Dr. Farley was one of the men; "but I chose another guy—a big one— and that's all I remember."

Therapist: Perhaps your feelings about Dr. Farley's leaving have something to do with your feelings about not wanting to come.

Sam: Nah, Dr. Farley finished his apprenticeship and went out to make money.

Therapist: And you didn't even get to choose a new therapist from a lineup?

Sam: (Laughing) Does Dr. Farley have his office around here? And how much more money is he going to make? He didn't stay here very long.

Therapist: (I'm beginning to feel uncomfortable . . .) I wonder if you're asking how I compare to Dr. Farley and what kind of a guy I am.

Sam: Yeah. Are you in your apprenticeship, too?

Therapist: You mean: Will I be leaving also?

Sam: Why should you stay here if you can make more money seeing people in private?

Therapist: (Now, I'm really uncomfortable!) And why should you want to come to see a man who's just going to leave you when you get to know him?

Sam: I don't like that! I've never forgiven my dad for that divorce. He's stupid.

Therapist: Then you have a real reason to get angry at men who leave you. I understand your being mad at Dr. Farley and I can even understand that you would be angry at me if you thought I might leave.

Sam: Are you going to leave, too? I don't mean like for your vacation, but not to be here any more?

Therapist: No, Sam, I am here all of the time, and I plan to stay.

Sam: Don't you want to make more money?

Therapist: Each adult decides what kinds of things he likes best in his work, and I like best doing the things I do here.

Sam: (Laughs) Maybe you're some kind of a nut who doesn't like money, but it's good to know you aren't going to leave in a couple of months.

Therapist: What's really good to know is that you don't have to be angry at me about something that you only *thought* might happen instead of having a good, real reason to be mad at me.

Near the end of the hour, Sam described his fury and disappointment at his father's continually broken promises. I agreed that this was a real reason for feeling angry. When he asked to smoke, I told him that he was the one to decide what he does during our hours together. Leaving, he told me he would see me next week—"same time and station." He made no further mention of stopping treatment, and I didn't broach the subject.

Two minutes after his departure, he returned to the door and said,

"You know, I really was mad at Dr. Farley"—and left without waiting for a response.

Discussion

Although Sam's first therapist felt that his impact on the boy had been minimal, it had, in fact, been a more important relationship than the therapist had credited. Not only was it important in its own right, but, additionally, the relationship and its ending rekindled memories of an earlier series of disappointments with and loss of his father.

In the brief account of the first two post-transfer hours, the therapist notes how different Sam's behavior is from how he acted with Dr. Farley. In those hours, he talks incessantly, denying any hurt or disappointment, behind a façade of pseudo-sophistication and fantasies of impenetrability and magical power. While seemingly making "common cause" with his new therapist, Sam can express old angers but not the more recent rage at Dr. Farley. The only clue to his ambivalent hostility toward Dr. Farley is in Sam's veiled sarcasm about his appreciation of Dr. Farley's realistic decision to finish training and go out and get rich.

The current therapist's willingness to listen and wait without challenging the defensive bravado finally pays off in the third session. The dream reveals Sam's readiness to tackle directly his feelings of loss and anger with Dr. Farley. The new therapist quickly sees the opportunity and skillfully weaves the discussion around the transfer, the affects it has stirred up, and their relationship to his history and ongoing problems.

This therapist has the advantage of knowing that he has no plans to leave since he is a new member of a clinic staff. Despite this reality, the therapist is aware of his discomfort in offering Sam a sense of stability which outdoes the previous therapist. Had this therapist been a trainee with a known, time-limited stay at the agency, the issue would have been far trickier and perhaps unresolvable.

The next two cases illustrate the ending of a period of psychotherapy in which a transfer is clearly being considered. As such, this phase of the work must serve two simultaneous purposes:

1) As gracefully as possible, some closure to this period of work must be achieved and, in a sense, the prior time of therapy must stand on its own merits. Inherent in any incomplete psychotherapeutic work are a sense of loss and a sense of unfinished business shared by both parties. Some resolution of the unique relationship which has existed between the two people must occur, even though both are aware that further therapy with a new therapist will go on. If the work has gone well, it has its own unique resolution as well as serving as a recapitulation of earlier separations.

2) At one and the same time, transfer work prepares the patient to yield the old relationship with enough freedom to take on a new one.

We will be able to review how the two objectives were approached and handled by the departing therapist in each illustrative case. The reader may want to imagine that he or she is to be the next therapist and consider how he or she might initiate and continue the therapeutic work with each of these youngsters. For this imaginery exercise, we suggest a few notes of caution. Beginning therapists naturally want to do well. Sometimes this promotes an unintended competitive stance vis-à-vis the prior therapist, who may or may not be known to you. Doing well is not necessarily the same as outdoing one's colleague.

It is frequently more difficult to experience a transferred "case" as one's own. On occasion, the new therapist attempts to take proprietary rights over the patient by moving too quickly without sufficient attention to the transition and the possible "mourning-work" which must not be short-circuited. An opposite tendency is the temptation to take everything the prior therapist offers as gospel—to resist doing your own assessment of the patient's current status and continuing needs. This is frequently manifested by the new therapist's interpreting everything the patient says as symbolically related to the old therapist. Sometimes, even transferred patients have new problems!

Case 3—Martha

Martha is 16 and has been in treatment for 18 months on a once-weekly basis. Around the time that her therapist announced that he would be leaving the clinic, he also suggested that she see her neurologist for a reevaluation of her epilepsy. She agreed to do this. The therapist's account of the last weeks of his work with Martha begins with the first session after her neurologic exam:

Martha arrived at my office in a state of sullen fury. She complained bitterly about Dr. Harris (the neurologist), commenting that he was "a son of a bitch." She had seen him in the clinic, because her parents couldn't afford to send her to his private office. Dr. Harris had been nowhere as nice as he'd been during their first appointment, Martha said, and he had treated her as if "he didn't give a damn about me. I guess the money we paid at his office made all the difference," she further surmised. She felt humiliated to have been a "charity case."

I asked what had transpired during the visit, but there seemed nothing specific, aside from the physician's business-like demeanor, to account for her anger. I suggested that perhaps Dr. Harris had the dubious honor of absorbing some of her feelings about me. Her response was quick denial, then, "Why should I be angry with you? You weren't responsible for what happened with Dr. Harris. You didn't send me to the clinic." I replied that, on the contrary, I had, since it was at my urging she had contacted him for the appointment. Martha then returned to what had happened with Dr. Harris. He had asked if she were still seeing me, and she had responded by bursting into tears. After all, she'd known for several months that I would be leaving in June.

I wondered where she imagined I'd go. She said she figured I would open a plush office in Pacific Heights, and she knew she could never afford the prices I would charge; she then blandly commented that she expected this and understood: "That's the economics of life." When I pointed out to her how "well" she was accepting this idea— as opposed to how bitter she was about coming to the clinic to see Dr. Harris—she began to see the point and acknowledged that she had been angry with me for some time. "It's kind of been in the background, though," she mused, "but, yeah, you know, maybe you're right; maybe I am pissed at you for leaving." A sullen silence followed. I asked her if she'd thought of asking me where I was going.

She said the question had crossed her mind but that she hadn't gotten around to asking. "But I don't want to know, so don't tell me."

The hour ended, and she left in great haste, closing the door with a perceptible slam.

During our next meeting, Martha talked little and looked glum. She had been "down" the whole week, she said, and complained about school and how hard it was for her to finish things. "This, too, maybe?" I suggested. She answered with annoyance: "Oh, Dr. Brown, you think everything has to do with therapy," then showed a slight smile. For a time she was quiet, but I then asked, "Do you remember what you said at the end of the last session?"

Martha: No, uh . . . yeah, you mean about my not wanting to know where you're going? I don't want to know because it might hurt to know.

Therapist: How would it hurt?

Martha: Oh, I guess I would feel sort of rejected if I knew for sure you were going to open an office in Pacific Heights—like I wasn't important enough to you that you would continue seeing me in your private office.

While we pursued this idea, she said she didn't see how she could stand another rejection from someone she considered important. I wondered with her whether the fantasy about something is not sometimes worse than the reality. She replied astutely, "That's the way it was with lots of other things we talked about."

I commented, "Maybe this, too?"

"Maybe this, too," replied steadily. "Where are you going, anyway?"

"I have to go into the Army."

She smiled, with a great expression of relief. "I really made a mountain out of a molehill that time!"

Somehow, telling her that I had to go into the Army made all the difference. "There's no rejection, because it's not my choice?"

"Yeah, that's it. Boy, do I ever feel better about it now."

The hour ended, and she said—smiling widely as she reached the door, "See you next week, Shrink."

In the weeks that followed, Martha was able to discuss how she had felt about me during the treatment. She admitted to having had a "crush" on me from time to time in the past but said she was always too embarrassed to talk about it. "Anyway, you probably knew all along," she guessed. Somehow it was easier to be angry with me. Being able to express both sides of the ambivalence allowed her to begin disengaging herself from me. She expressed an interest in continuing treatment—partly out of a fear that her symptoms might return, but also because of her realization that she still had trouble relating to people. She was aware of her exaggerated fear that if she became close to someone, he would disappoint her. However, she was even more fearful that *she* would disappoint the person. We then discussed some of these anxieties in the context of the potential new therapist. When I first broached the idea that she might have a female worker, Martha's first reaction was, "Oh no, I couldn't talk to a woman like I talk to you." Neither could she *feel* about a woman like she could about a man. . . .

Martha was preoccupied with the idea of people replacing each other. Having seen her natural father three weeks before treatment ended, she at first felt euphoric about what a nice guy he was and about how much he resembled me, physically and emotionally. She said I was a father substitute, and now that she had him, she could substitute him back for me. During the final week, she reconsidered this idea and began to feel that neither of us substituted for the other. She didn't think she needed to think of us in that way any longer.

Two sessions prior to termination, she expressed an interest in whether or not I planned to return to the Bay Area after the Army. She said she had the image of herself all grown up and mature by then, and would be able to see me in treatment again.

Discussion

This youngster shows us how hard it is to be disappointed by people who are important to her. In the history, we learn that she was left by her own father, which fact may account for a) displaced anger regarding termination (from the therapist to Dr. Harris)— anger emanating, in part, from her father's original departure; and

b) fantasized certainty that she is the object of rejection—resulting in the construction of a whole "fantasy-reality" about how "no one could give a damn" about her. She would almost prefer this imagined scenario to the actual events and reality issues of her life.

Just how Martha's subjective reality is filtered through previous experiences forms the foundation for the transference-loaded hours reported above. The pace and process of this transference-talk involve anger expressed obliquely through another event and a retentive silence—anger at the neurologist to protect the therapist. She slams the door—"I am leaving you!"—when the reverse is more nearly accurate. Some depression follows this realization: "Am I worthless?" she wonders. Perhaps people for whom she feels emotional attachment leave her gladly!

After expressing a measure of her anger and grief, she begins to work on the reality events and their meaning to her. Perhaps the lost object (therapist) can be expediently replaced by another—in this case, the father, her original loss. Yet this "solution" is a wish; in fact, she learns that people are not really replaceable and interchangeable. This may free her to engage in a meaningful relationship with her new therapist.

Thus, she can address the future and wonder: What will the "new one" be like? . . . Well, he/she can't be as good. A retrospective view of the relationship between Martha and her therapist reveals that they, too, have a history in common. Perhaps they will reunite after he finishes with the Army and she leaves adolescence. Regrets continue and cannot be wiped out. It is hardly necessary to belabor the meanings of this wish to restore the relationship at some future date. Suffice it to say that it probably means to Martha something other than a simple resumption of psychotherapy with a professionally esteemed therapist.

Case 4—Stuart

Identifying Data. Stuart is a nine-year-old boy: short, stocky and dull-appearing, with prominent teeth, wide brown eyes, and a frightened-looking demeanor. Stuart has a brother, aged four.

Application to the clinic was made by the mother when Stuart was eight. Her chief complaints were his withholding of bowel movements, his emotional immaturity, his fear of playing with boys his own age, his tantrums, bedwetting, nightmares and occasional cessation of talking. The mother was concurrently seeking help for herself.

Family Constellation. Mother, age 33, was seen by Stuart's therapist every month and had improved considerably. Father, age 48, was separated from the family from the time Stuart was five years, two months, until just recently, when he began visiting the family every Sunday.

Course of Therapy. Throughout his therapy, Stuart has consistently played games and only occasionally spoken with me. He responded to my questions and statements by saying nothing or by giving me frightened looks or monosyllabic answers. After the initial months, I began to interpret his silence and reticence.

In each game, his conflict over bigness and smallness became apparent; this, too, was interpreted to him. As a result, Stuart became somewhat more expressive. After six months, I began to see him twice a week, and a most gratifying and noticeable response was his increased ability to talk as well as to display affects—aggression and affection, particularly. He became increasingly active in these hours and told me he was going to save a lot of money and buy various things.

Anticipating that my departure from the clinic would be a difficult time for him in light of the loss of his father, I told him in April that I would be leaving in June. Around this time, his mother reported being extremely delighted at how much her son had changed during the past year. He was much more sociable, getting better marks in school and participating in sports. She noted that, even at home, he was being quite helpful to the little girl upstairs who also had no father. In May and June, as my departure became more imminent, Stuart began to be increasingly curious about me.

The following hour occurred after I missed an hour because of a trip. We played for a bit, and then we had the following exchange:

Stuart: My friend, Alex, is going to New York.
Therapist: Like I did?

Stuart: I was born in New York. Where were you born?

Therapist: Wyoming.

Stuart: Is that near New York?

Therapist: Well, it's about 2,000 miles away. Are you remembering that I'll be leaving soon?

Stuart: No.

Therapist: Well, as I told you, in June I will be going.

Stuart: To New York?

Therapist: No, to Berkeley.

Stuart: Will you send me a postcard?

Therapist: Like I did from New York?

Stuart: Yes.

Therapist: Sure I will.

Stuart then went into a long discussion about the roll of scotch tape which was on my desk and wanted to know how long it was.

Therapist: Not quite far enough to reach to Berkeley.

Stuart: Well, it must be pretty long. Will it stretch across the desk?

Therapist: Sure.

Stuart then pulled the whole piece of tape across my desk. He asked me to hold one end as he held the other and stretched it. "This is like keeping us hooked together across a long distance, isn't it?" I asked. He made no response but wanted to know if the tape would hold on the top of the desk in case of fire. I wondered what made him think of that. Again, no answer.

Stuart: I can't pull the top of the desk off, but I know somebody who can. Guess who?

Therapist: Superman?

Stuart: That's me. (Begins to show me some karate and judo holds.)

Therapist: If you were Superman, you could jump right across to Berkeley in nothing flat, couldn't you? Superman can fly.

He made no comment on this statement but asked, instead, if I would teach him some judo chops. We then took up the pick-up sticks, and he proceeded to break the whole box. I commented on his possible anger. No response. At the end of the hour, he left with a smile and a bounce.

In the succeeding hours, Stuart expressed a great deal of curiosity about me. He wanted to know if I was in the Army, whether I had learned to fight, how old I was, where I was born, and where I went to school. He expressed a great deal of surprise when I told him I had gone to the same school for 12 years. Armed with this remarkable report of scholastic stability, he immediately told me about his father: Father had just had a 48th birthday, and Stuart had given him 48 spanks and a new shirt, and father had taken him to Golden Gate Park.

Next hour, we compared strength by seeing who could open up the glue jar. Again, Stuart became quite curious about me and also about the calendar on my desk. Looking at the calendar, he said he would be 14 in 1981, and I asked if he was wondering about the future and what would happen when I was gone. He made no answer but began immediately to talk, rather, of Mars and of how people might go there soon.

Therapist: Is that where people go when they leave?

Stuart: I don't know. (Stuart then asked again where I lived. I told him.)

Stuart: That's not so far.

Therapist: You don't think it's too far for me to keep coming here?

Stuart: No.

He then became agitated and began tossing my keys around (he'd been playing with them) and hiding the toy soldiers. I asked him if in hiding the soldiers, he was wondering where old Navy men, like me, go when you don't see them. He began to toss them around.

Therapist: It looks to me as if you're quite mad. (No response.) You're probably mad at me and mad at yourself at the same time, but mostly me. It's kind of tough to be mad at someone you like, isn't it?

With this, he gave me a nasty look. Although time was up, he wanted to stay longer. He did. I suggested we clean up the mess he had made. He picked up a few of the soldiers, then slid down the bannister and disappeared.

During the next hour, the continued theme of his anger and upset surfaced again, as he tossed a rubber knife back and forth and then had me toss it at him. I repeatedly interpreted his anger at me and at himself, along with his attachment for me.

In the next two hours, Stuart showed me some Navy pennant cards which were used to send messages across the waves. I repeatedly interpreted to him, as he was teaching me, that if I were able to learn the signals, we would be able to send messages across the water like the Navy does or across the Bay between here and Berkeley. At this, he merely smiled; but he expressed amazement when I was able to correctly name some of the Navy pennants. He also wanted to learn how to play "bridge," and I began to teach him. We played "bridge": He would make books and set them up cross-wise, informing me that he was making a bridge. "Like between here and Berkeley?" I asked—to which he made no response except to ask where Berkeley was. I drew him a map. He said he thought it would be a good idea for his father to take him over there some day so he could look at Berkeley.

Stuart repeated some of his previous concerns during our last hour together. Expressing curiosity about the new therapist, he wanted to know if he would be able to play poker. I said I didn't know, but that Stuart could teach him. My departing gift to him was a deck of cards and the map I had drawn.

Discussion

This retentive little boy has obviously made considerable progress in treatment. In the beginning, he "saves" words, feelings and bowel movements. Although this "holding on" style continues—he "saves" money, cards, and still responds sparingly—it is obvious that some freeing-up has occurred. This is evident in the interviews, in his behavior at school and at home, and from the mother's account.

This progress allows Stuart and his therapist to work productively on an important event—the therapist's imminent departure and his transfer to a new therapist. The theme of loss emerges in direct discussion, in metaphorical conversation, and in the play. Bridges, cards, scotch tape, and Navy pennants are transparent efforts to convey the loss and the wish to maintain connections. Superman and other manifestations of strength and power, like opening the glue jar, are defensive efforts to cope with a sense of helplessness. Stuart also attempts to deal with this more realistically in his questions about time, space and geography. This demonstrates his increased ability to express curiosity and to acquire new information. This is undoubtedly part of the explanation for the improvement in his school work. In his real world, he has recently reestablished connection with his father, which should help him to manage his therapist's leaving more effectively. We note his plan to have his father help him "check out Berkeley."

Throughout the reported hours, the therapist steadfastly interprets the direct and metaphorical material, as related to the coming separation and Stuart's feelings about it. While Stuart initially denies that he is thinking about this, his behavior and responses increasingly demonstrate that he is indeed concerned and actively coping with the issues. Sufficient work is accomplished regarding the loss so that Stuart is enabled to turn his attention to the future, which includes a new therapist. The therapist's two gifts are symbolic of their common activity, thus maintaining an important connection, but also creating a link with the new therapist. "Here's a deck of cards, with which you can teach your new therapist poker."

The new therapist should not expect the issue of Stuart's recent termination to "blossom" as a prime topic of discussion during the early hours. Often, such matters emerge much more slowly. This is particularly likely in view of Stuart's reticent character style. The zealous assumption that Stuart will want to discuss his old therapist immediately may risk more intrusiveness than Stuart can manage. Much careful groundwork, including developing a new relationship well fortified with trust, must precede the reemergence of this painful material.

VACATIONS

Brief interruptions will occur in all therapeutic work. The most common of these are vacation periods which sometimes stimulate and bring to the surface latent anxieties about object constancy and object loss. While one does not plan therapeutic interruptions in order to provoke work on these conflicts, their natural occurrence can provide the opportunity to help a child with these. As with transfers, pre- and post-work should occur around a vacation. In contrast to transfers, the same therapist has an opportunity to observe the child's management of a disruption in the relationship. To illustrate, we will present the case of Frank.

Frank

Frank is seven. He is the son of Chinese-American parents who were divorced when he was two and a half. A second grader in a Catholic school, Frank lives at home with his mother, his maternal grandparents, and a maternal uncle. His mother is a severely disturbed woman given to capricious outbursts, oscillating betwen overly guilty and overly gratifying behavior toward Frank. Shortly before Frank's visit to the clinic, his mother packed Frank's things in a suitcase and threatened to send him away. Such threats of separation and loss are central to his life.

While Frank is a bright, charming child with good imagination and lots of energy, his depression is apparent, just below the surface. Frank was referred to the clinic for erratic school performance and daydreaming.

The following are two pre-vacation sessions with Frank:

During the eighteenth week of our once-weekly appointments, I tell Frank that I will be going on a two-week vacation three weeks hence. On the calendar, I show him when this will be and when I will return. He says, "OK," and turns to the toy cabinet, from which he pulls the frequently used puppets and a magnifying glass.

With Frank's accompanying noisy sounds, the bear sticks out his tongue. There is much laughter when the bear throws two balls at once at the monkeys—often a representation of Frank—who try to catch the balls but fail.

Suddenly, the bear and the dog are pronounced dead—this in rapid-fire fashion. A doctor is called to listen to their heartbeats, while the monkeys are told to pray. The doctor listens to the heartbeats and acknowledges that the bear and dog are—miraculously—alive again.

Frank comments that the bear is mean and can protect himself, while the dog stays in the house. I ask what this is all about. Instead of replying, Franks finds the flashlight. It doesn't work; when I observe this, he says, "That's OK."

Then he turns to my curtains and says that he wants to nail them down; he wants to fix them. I ask if he's nailed other things before. He replies that, recently, he nailed wheels to his friend's wagon. When he asks for nails, I tell him that I can have some for him next week.

Leaving the curtains, Frank builds a fort and sets army men inside. As he tries to pile the men into trucks, his play becomes more and more chaotic, and I observe how hurried he is. He tells me there is too little time and he must hurry.

Noticing some pictures of mountains on my wall, he says, "Looks like mountains . . . . Last time you told me you were going to the mountains on vacation."

I replied, "It's this week I told you I'll be going on vacation. Maybe you're unhappy that I'm going to be gone?"

"No," said Frank, "I like people to have a good time on vacation."

Frank limps in to our next session—his ankle hurts. I look at his ankle and find out what happened. He turns to the magnifying glass and tells me that we are to hide little things and find them. He moves the magnifying glass to his own eye, comments on how things look bigger and smaller and then brings it to my eye. "Your eye is big . . . It's scary."

At this point, he asks if I have brought him things to bang. I had not. Turning to the puppets, he chooses the bear, which begins to throw a ball that he calls a rotten tomato.

I comment that the bear seems to be in a bad mood. Meanwhile, the dog pretends to whisper to the monkeys but quickly begins, instead, to spit and to hit them. Taking the role of the monkeys, I ask what this is about. The dog replies that the monkeys are mean, stupid and bad. Frank throws the puppets at me. Immediately, he must go to the bathroom.

More quietly, he returns and takes out the paints. He carefully begins to reproduce the paintbox itself in a painting and talks about being happy to go back to school: He will have physical education— not homework. I tell him that I know from his mother that sometimes he does his homework and sometimes he doesn't. "Yes," he says, "my hand hurts."

I acknowledge that mother gets angry when he doesn't do his

homework. He agrees and tells me that mother loses her temper and sometimes hits with a belt. I ask how he feels when this happens. "Very sad . . . because it hurts a lot," he replies.

It is time to end the hour, and I mention my vacation again. Frank asks where I'll go, and I offer to send a postcard—telling him that I'll be going to New York.

"Be careful," he says, "of King Kong and of the monster who lives a thousand years."

I assure him that I will be safe.

Post-Vacation Hour. Frank arrives on time, and in an apparently chipper mood. He goes immediately to the toy cabinet and takes out the monkeys, bear and the dog. Though I had placed Frank's painting prominently on the desk, he scrupulously ignores it for the entire session. His play is rapid-fire, with occasional orders to me to get him what he requires.

The monkeys, bear and dog are involved in a highly confused fight, accompanied by lots of noise and giggling. The monkeys are once again labeled as "stupid and mean," with the bear giving them orders to "shape up."

I ask Frank whether he got my postcard. He stops fleetingly, but does not answer. He returns to the play but very soon thereafter says, "The bear is not in a bad mood, like he was last week." I say, "But the monkeys are still mean and stupid." Frank says, "Yeah, they're always stupid but the bear will play with them today, anyway."

Toward the end of the hour, I try to introduce a discussion of my vacation and how things had been for him when we did not see one another. Frank ignores my comments completely. However, as he leaves, he says over his shoulder, "I still want those nails!"

Discussion

Although Frank's verbal responses to the therapist's vacation announcement are spare, his play richly demonstrates his awareness of the coming separation. His anger and hurt appear again and again in the animal play and in his hurt ankle and hand. The animals die suddenly and incomprehensibly in the course of game, to be magically resurrected by a doctor.

He tries to "nail things down," but there are no supplies to accomplish this. Efforts to build a fort become chaotic and he conveys his pressure by announcing that he is forced to hurry since there is too little time. The therapist's picture of mountains stimulates his first verbal comment about the therapist's vacation, in which he distorts the amount of notice that he has been given.

In the second hour, Frank's increasing anger and apprehension are evident. The animals fight once again, perceptions become "scary," and, as he experiences greater anger with the therapist, he becomes frightened of his own feelings and must leave the room. Attempting restitution, he paints an exact "replica" of the paint box, and, following the therapist's offer to send a postcard, he warns her about dangers and the need to be cautious.

The therapist's interventions help this boy to express some of his feelings and to see their relationship to the stress of the vacation. Through her verbal statements, but, far more profoundly, through her calm, sturdy stance, she attempts to convey that both of them can weather the separation safely. These efforts are, understandably, only partly successful, in light of this boy's experiences.

Following the vacation, Frank must ignore the disruption. He cannot acknowledge his picture or the postcard he received. He resists any direct discussion of the vacation and wipes out the time interval between the sessions. However, in the metaphor of play, he can pick up prior themes, and avow that this time the bear's mood has improved and that the bear will play with the "stupid" monkeys anyway.

His parting "shot" reminds us that unfinished business remains and that he is prepared to continue the work.

11

Understanding and
Working with Parents

Any effort to understand parents and to work with them in conjunction with the treatment of a child must begin with an appreciation of parenthood as a development stage and a developmental process. It is only in recent years that we have come to understand the psychology of parenthood in this way. There is a growing body of information and literature about parenthood, the variations in parental styles, and the reciprocal needs and relationship between parents and their children. Our current understanding rejects the "tabula rasa" view of the child in favor of a more sophisticated and complex conception of a dynamic interplay between parent and child. Each parent and each child have different "sending and receiving" capacities which influence and build upon one another over time. This reciprocity, however, is not equal for the child and the parents. At first the child's need is absolute, whereas a parent's need is, typically, only relative. Later this balance shifts, requiring the parent to modulate caretaking responses in the face of the child's growing independence. Ill-timed or otherwise inappropriate modulations in this relationship will impair the growth of both child and parent.

This complex and changing perspective is further complicated by current social and cultural changes within our society. Perhaps nowhere are these changes more evident than in the conduct of family

181

life. The task of parenthood, previously considered a responsibility as a mere matter of course, is changing greatly in the face of changing values, changing sex roles, high divorce rates, increasingly large numbers of single-parent families, and high mobility rates. The norm is no longer the rule; guidelines for parents, once available through one's own heritage, community, neighborhood and friends, are no longer as relevant in today's rapidly shifting scene.

One event in parenthood which is particularly difficult is the decision to seek help for a child. Often parents delay seeking help in the hope that the child's symptoms and suffering are simply a passing phase. On occasion, this is so; however, just as often, it is *not* the case and the stigma associated with applying for psychiatric services accounts for parental delay. Almost every parent will come to the decision to seek help with struggle and pain. The parent is faced with the acknowledgment that the family itself can no longer adequately cope with and manage the child's problems. Such acknowledgment is inevitably accompanied by guilt, shame, helplessness, bewilderment and anger. For some parents, these feelings are so powerful as to be intolerable. They must be denied and extruded, often through the mechanisms of seeking some external source upon which to project blame. Such parents often come, if at all, at the behest of some authority—the school, Court, physician—and have great difficulty in forming an alliance with the therapist. They may displace upon the therapist the feelings associated with the resisted authority.

However, even such highly resistant parents may come to experience the therapist differently, if sufficient respect and tact are offered for the parents' suffering. Whether vividly portrayed or not, the suffering will be present in almost every parent who seeks help for his child. It is easy for the beginning therapist to lose sight of this with those parents who are less conflicted and who appear more motivated and cooperative.

We can neither rescue children, nor hope to accomplish for them the tasks that rightfully belong to the family. Our aim is to help children and families utilize their own resources more effectively, so that they can live with one another in greater harmony.

As indicated earlier, work with parents has three major objectives:

1) The maintenance of an alliance with the family for the continued support of the child's treatment;
2) The obtaining of a continual flow of pertinent information about the child's ongoing life; and
3) The common task of parent and therapist to create or modify those aspects of the child's outer world which may either fuel the disturbance or affect the child's growth.

The following vignettes from work with parents illustrate various aspects of how the work addresses one or another of these objectives.

MAINTAINING THE ALLIANCE

Mr. and Mrs. Clarke have four children. Philip is their third, aged nine at the time of referral. Philip is underachieving in school, has increasingly been involved in fights with schoolmates, is defiant at home and "shuts himself off from the whole family." The Clarke household is full of strife. Mr. Clarke and his wife bicker constantly, usually about the father's emotional distance which cannot satisfy his wife's neediness. The more she tugs—the more he pulls away. Philip has always been considered Mrs. Clarke's special child, and she finds his increasing withdrawal more and more intolerable. She has responded to this withdrawal by escalating her efforts to involve herself in all aspects of Philip's life. He repeatedly "sends messages" for her to "lay-off," leaving her increasingly bewildered and "walking on eggs" with him.

Philip experiences the treatment referral as another example of the mother's intrusiveness and resists coming to his hours. Yet when he does come, therapeutic work proceeds. As might be expected, Mrs. Clarke grows increasingly upset about Philip's complaints about continuing therapy and responds with uncertainty about insisting that he continue. In addition, she also attempts to interpret, to him, the psychological meaning of his resistance and to plead with him to understand her reasons for sending him.

The therapist recognizes this mother's difficulty in firmly insisting on Philip's regular attendance and in leaving the interpretations about Philip's resistance to the therapist. Although there are many complicated psychological factors underlying this push-pull behavior, the therapist correctly decides that the first interventions must be aimed at protecting the child's treatment, and promoting the alliance with the mother by freeing Mrs. Clarke of the excess burdens of being both parent and psychotherapist. Simultaneously, she clarifies the importance of the mother's role and the distinctions between that important source of help for Philip and her own therapeutic work. Firmly, she advises the mother to insist that Philip come to his appointments and to encourage Philip to discuss his complaints about therapy with the therapist. She explains to Mrs. Clarke that Philip's resistance is one more manifestation of their push-pull relationship and helps Mrs. Clarke tolerate the distinction between their mutual efforts to help Philip. With this help, the mother is able to support the treatment with greater firmness, a firmness which, in fact, helps Philip feel more protected.

In this process, Mrs. Clarke is relieved of an unnecessary burden, can take on a more appropriate mothering role, with less vacillation, and utilizes the therapist's firmness as a model for her behavior. Everyone becomes less confused about tasks and roles and the therapeutic alliance with Mrs. Clarke and Philip is strengthened. In this instance, it was fortunate that the therapist's initial approach to "settling" this family into treatment was sufficient. If the advice and support given to Mrs. Clarke had been insufficient, the therapeutic task of forming a viable alliance would have been much more complicated. This might have involved a much longer and more complex approach aimed at interpreting Mrs. Clarke's displacement of the conflicted push-pull relationship with her husband onto her son and his treatment.

THE VALUE OF KEEPING UP-TO-DATE

Paula is a bright four-and-a-half-year-old child, who has been in psychotherapy for ten months because of severe phobic symptoms, which began shortly after her third birthday and which had markedly limited her activities and development. Paula has improved considerably. Her phobic symptoms are much diminished. Her mother reported that Paula learned of her pregnancy without any apparent regression and with some apparent pleasure. Both Paula and her therapist learned of the mother's pregnancy approximately four weeks before the following events occurred in the playroom.

For two consecutive sessions, Paula busily arranged all the chairs in a tight cluster, bound them together with string, and covered the entire construction with paper. She left a small opening and crawled in and out with some nervous giggling. Armed with his knowledge of the pregnancy, the therapist "understood" the play as a symbolic acting out of fantasies about pregnancy and birth. After making some observations to Paula about her manifest behavior, her pleasure and her "worried" giggle, he considers the best way of interpreting to her his "certain" interpretation of its latent meaning. However, since the second of these sessions is about to end, he decides to wait to deliver his interpretation until next week. In the intervening week, he meets with Paula's parents in a regularly scheduled interview. They tell him that three weeks earlier, the family had gone camping. They were very pleased that Paula was able to manage this experience without significant fears and say, "that's something she couldn't have done a few months ago." They did note that she was a bit anxious about sleeping in a tent with them and her older brother, but she was easily reassured.

Though the therapist realizes that his "pregnancy-fantasy" interpretation is probably also correct, it is quite clear now that the play behavior refers more immediately to the recent tent experience and that these issues should be taken up first.

Keeping up-to-date with events of a child's daily life is particularly important with young children. Without ongoing knowledge of the child's real world, the therapist's field of understanding and interventions narrows unnecessarily.

GIVING EXPLANATIONS, INFORMATION AND ADVICE

It is possible and desirable, in some situations, to provide parents with an explanation of the child's behavior and a straightforward piece of advice. As indicated, the therapist's impressions of the child and his behavior can be conveyed to the parent without violating the strict rules of confidentiality. Such impressions often help a parent gain some perspective and some distance from the child's problems. Behavior which may have been seen as intentionally thwarting the parent can sometimes be seen in a new light, particularly if the parent recognizes that he is not being blamed. The giving of such information is predicated on the understanding of the parent's capacity to assimilate the information and use it productively.

Similarly, the giving of advice must not rest solely on what the child requires, but on whether the parent can use the advice. Advice which falls directly into the parent's area of conflict is unlikely to be heard and utilized. It may, in fact, engender more guilt and difficulty. The therapist must have some certainty that the parent is lacking in knowledge rather than immobilized by conflict.

To illustrate, we can consider the case of Mary:

Mary, age seven, began having temper tantrums after learning that her parents had decided to separate. During the initial play session, she told the therapist her biggest fear—she was worried that when her parents separated she would have to choose which parent she would live with. Her fear was that whichever one she did not choose would be very mad at her. Her temper tantrums clearly displayed her own anger with an unchosen set of circumstances. Both parents were advised to make it plain that Mary would not be forced to choose. They let her know clearly and firmly that the responsibility for deciding on appropriate living and visiting would be theirs and that they would make sure that she would remain in contact with both. They had not appreciated her worry and utilized the advice straightforwardly. Mary's temper outbursts receded.

In this instance, the symptom and its context were clarified in a way that the parents could understand, thus freeing them to address Mary's worry and her underlying concern that the separation would leave her unprotected and unilaterally abandoned.

On the other hand, Mrs. Fraser, a rather disturbed and disorganized mother, informed the therapist, during the first evaluation interview, that she and her 12-year-old son shared the same bed. Alert to theoretical consequences of this overly close relationship, the therapist immediately advised Mrs. Fraser that this practice contributed to a child's difficulty and urged her to change sleeping arrangements. This "good" advice startled the mother and led to a series of broken appointments. Repeated efforts to reestablish contact following a careful review of the first hour failed. The review revealed a long-standing symbiotic tie between Mrs. Fraser and her son. It is entirely probable that the therapist's premature and incomplete understanding of her needs, as well as the child's, led to the disruption.

MODIFYING INTERACTIONS

Thirteen-year-old James is a deeply disturbed boy. He is an only child referred for incessant worry, isolation and vague somatic complaints. His fears are pervasive and confused; any issue can quickly be converted into an impending catastrophe. The parents are strict and hard taskmasters. The family's rules of conduct are endless, complicated and often confusing. The father, in particular, has many complicated rules about eating, sleeping, appropriate dress, and health management which he presents to James dogmatically and without much explanation. This further confuses James and adds to his fears that the world is endlessly fraught with danger.

The therapist recognizes that her efforts to help James understand the world in a more rational way cannot succeed unless the parents and, particularly the father, modify their expectations and behavior. The father reluctantly agrees to participate in the parent meetings. The therapist's tentative first efforts to explore with the parents the possibility of altering their approach to James is countered by the father's response: "I'm set in my ways and I can't change." The therapist does not persist in urging that the father consider changing, recognizing that he feels too threatened by such an idea. Instead, she explores with him the efficacy of his present efforts to get James to measure up. In effect, her attention is centered on what the mother, and, particularly, the father do with James, and whether these efforts are successful in achieving their objectives. In this process, the father can acknowledge that some of his efforts do not, in fact, achieve his aims. Each such acknowledgment is usually followed by some variation of the father's theme, "But, I can't change." Despite this, the therapist begins to hear from James and from the mother that the father is modifying his behavior. He is yelling less and is more temperate in his demands. The therapist carefully avoids confronting the father with the evidence of his actual changed behavior, though the temptation to do so is nearly irresistible. She permits him to continue with his insistence that it is impossible for him to change. Instead, the exploration of current interactions and their practical outcomes remains her sole focus.

The work with these parents did not simply derive from a trial and error approach. It rested, instead, on a careful appraisal of James and his family. The therapist learned during the evaluation that James' father had recently suffered a variety of setbacks. A heart attack had led to a forced and premature retirement. Father's concern about his health, changed economic circumstances, and his altered life-style make it imperative that he try to maintain a sense that things are as they were. Furthermore, an acknowledgment of change might surface for the father the possibility that he might have contributed to James' difficulties. This understanding from the history is confirmed by the father's vehement response to the therapist's initial tentative exploration about whether the father could alter some of his behavior with James. The therapist correctly recognizes that a direct acknowledgment is out of the question. Instead, she allies herself with the father's appreciation for simple, practical and effective approaches to solving problems. In effect, she explores the possibility of whether he can modify small interactions with more successful outcomes, while maintaining the necessary inner defense against acknowledging change. This approach limits the area of work with the parents to those interactions with the child which contribute to his disturbance and which run counter to the therapist's approach to the child: It makes no effort to explore with the parents the etiology of the child's disturbance or the parental role in maintaining it, and, it recognizes the parents' genuine interest and concern for their son and focuses on their strengths. By respecting the parents' appreciation of the practical and the sensible, the therapist helps them to help their son without stripping them of their pride.

CARRYING "NO BLAMING" TOO FAR

Louis is 10, an only child who began psychotherapy because of learning difficulties and an inability to relate to peers. He has never known his father. His mother, Mrs. MacArthur, is a successful executive, whose work often involves travel at her choice. Louis had a year's treatment with one therapist, who left following his training. During the summer before he began work with his second therapist, Louis visited with an uncle and his family, who lived a considerable distance away. The mother's decision to send Louis to his uncle was made with the rationalization that it would be good for him to make the trip. Though Louis' former therapist questioned such an extended stay away from his mother, Mrs. MacArthur proceeded, nevertheless.

When Louis returned, there was considerable evidence that the stress of the separation had exacerbated his fearfulness—most characterized by an unwillingness to go out and play or leave his home generally. Mrs. MacArthur overreacted, became enormously solicitous, and yielded to many unreasonable demands by Louis. This is typical for her. Mrs. MacArthur's response to Louis oscillates between overconcerned reaction and a state of unmindfulness about his needs. In this instance, she impulsively considered leaving her job to spend all her time with Louis. However, as Louis' symptoms eased, she abandoned this plan—clearly relieved by the new therapist's agreement that it would have been an impossible burden for her.

A month or two later, Mrs. MacArthur reported that she had been on a brief trip again. The therapist was aware that these trips so soon after Louis' increased difficulties were not in the boy's best interest, but felt unable to say so. He decided that since the trip was past, there was no point in discussing it, and supported this conclusion with the idea that he must avoid confronting her, since it was important to develop and maintain a "good working alliance." For similar reason, he had not taken up the issue of a $150 unpaid bill.

The following week, Mrs. MacArthur told the therapist that she had an opportunity to attend a business conference which would take her away from the city for a week. Her firm would pay most of the expenses and it would only cost her $125. Her only problem was how to tell Louis about this forthcoming trip. The therapist spent his time with her discussing the importance of preparing Louis in advance and suggesting ways Mrs. MacArthur might go about this. Once again, he was aware of his conviction that such trips are disruptive to Louis, but could not state this in a straightforward fashion. He rationalized that Mrs. MacArthur would experience such a statement as an accusation.

In this instance, the therapist is blocked from making an appropriate intervention by his own anger, which forces him to distort a sound principle about not blaming the parent. His "walking on eggs" style with the mother precludes the establishment of a true working alliance and leaves Louis unprotected. Similarly, it leaves the mother at the mercy of her own conflicted impulses, while leaving untested the opportunity to work with the mother to alter her patterns of behavior toward greater consistency. Both mother and therapist attend to the superficial pseudo-problem while the central issue is left untouched. While it is true that Mrs. MacArthur may feel unblamed, she and her son are left unhelped.

These vignettes illustrate some of the common complexities of working with parents in behalf of the child's treatment. While each of these illustrates one objective in parent work, such work rarely remains focused on one dimension alone. At different stages of the work, the emphases may shift, as one or another of the principal objectives assumes greater importance. Although the work with the parents, over time, may have its primary thrust toward a specific objective, alterations usually occur as the work proceeds.

For some parents, none of the aims of collateral work will be sufficient. If the parent-child interaction is excessively bound in parental conflicts, it may be impossible to help the parent change such behavior without the resolution of conflict through the parent's own personal psychotherapy. It is not uncommon for the collateral work with the child's therapist to lead the parent and the therapist to a recognition of the need for personal treatment for the parent. This confronts the therapist with the choice of continuing to treat the parent with a different focus or referring the parent to a colleague, while collateral work continues with the child's therapist. The decision is a difficult one, since some parents will feel rejected and confused about starting anew with someone else. Some therapists experience the simultaneous psychotherapy of parent and child as a burden; the principle of an equidistant relationship becomes too complicated, raising questions of loyalty pulls. Others are more comfortable with this arrangement and can remain alert to the potential hazards of contradictory information, transferences and countertransferences.

Finally, it bears repeating that psychotherapy cannot serve all children and their parents. Inevitably, every therapist will meet children in families who are insufficiently protected, cared for and even abused. Frequently, such children are placed in and out of the family or repeatedly moved from one setting to another. These are the children of parents who can neither care for them or relinquish them to the care of others. We have been trained to respect the sanctity of the familial bond. This perspective tempts us to try psychotherapy as the solution. It is rarely effective. These are the times when it would perhaps be wise to acknowledge parental and psychotherapeutic limitations in favor of providing a constant and nourishing setting for the child. Also, inevitably, every therapist will meet families who must have a sick child for their own equilibrium and those who cannot give up any portion of their child's care to another. Regardless of the style, skill or zeal of the child therapist, little will be accomplished through psychotherapeutic means. The limitation of psychotherapy is perhaps the most painful knowledge the beginning therapist must acquire.

FURTHER READING

Anthony, E. James and Benedek, Therese (Eds.), (1970), *Parenthood: Its Psychology and Psychopathology*. Boston: Little, Brown and Company.
Coleman, Robert W., Kris, Ernst and Provence, Sally (1953), The Study of Variations of Early Parental Attitudes: A Preliminary Report. *Psychoanalytic Study of the Child*, 8:20-47.
Cooper, Shirley (1974), Treatment of Parents. In: *American Handbook of Psychiatry*, Vol. II, New York: Basic Books.
Jackson, Don (1965), The Study of the Family. *Family Process*, 4:1-20.
Korner, Analiese (1961), The Parent Takes the Blame. *Social Casework*, 42:339-342.
Munichin, Salvatore, et al. (1967), *Families of the Slums*. New York: Basic Books.